Dear Adrian

Thanks for buying my two copies!!

Best wishes

Ken Kahn-Harris

This is a first edition of 1,500 and is numbered

0492 ✻

Notting Hill Editions is an independent British publisher. The company was founded by Tom Kremer (1930–2017), champion of innovation and the man responsible for popularising the Rubik's Cube.

After a successful business career in toy invention Tom decided, at the age of eighty, to engage his passion for literature. In a digital world where time is short and books are throwaway, Tom's aim was to restore the art of the essay, and to create exceptionally beautiful books that would be cherished.

Hailed as 'the shape of things to come', the family-run press brings to print the most surprising thinkers of past and present. In an era of information-overload, these collectible pocket-size books distil ideas that linger in the mind.

www.nottinghilleditions.com

Dr Keith Kahn-Harris is a writer and sociologist. He teaches at Leo Baeck College and Birkbeck College and is a Fellow of the Institute for Jewish Policy Research. The author of four books, his interests range from the British Jewish community to extreme metal music scenes. He has contributed to numerous publications including the *Guardian*, *New Humanist* and *Times Literary Supplement*.

DENIAL

The Unspeakable Truth

–

Keith Kahn-Harris

Notting Hill Editions

Published in 2018
by Notting Hill Editions Ltd
Mirefoot, Kendal, Cumbria LA8 9AB

Original design by FLOK Design, Berlin, Germany
Cover design by Plain Creative, Kendal.
Editor: George Miller
Typeset by CB editions, London

Printed and bound
by Memminger MedienCentrum, Memmingen, Germany

Copyright © 2018 by Keith Kahn-Harris

The right of Keith Kahn-Harris to be identified as the author of this work has been asserted in accordance with Section 77 of the Copyright, Designs and Patents Act 1998. All rights reserved

This book is sold subject to the condition that it shall not, by way of trade or otherwise, be lent, resold, hired out or otherwise circulated without the publisher's prior consent in any form of binding or cover other than that in which it is published and without a similar condition including this condition being imposed on the subsequent purchaser

A CIP record for this book
is available from the British Library

ISBN 978-1-910749-96-8
www.nottinghilleditions.com

Contents

– Preface –
vii

– 1 The Failure –
1

– 2 The Audacity of Denialism –
16

– 3 Doing Denialism –
43

– 4 The Gap –
65

– 5 Predicament and Pathos –
91

– 6 The Denier's Alternative –
109

– 7 The Post-Denialist Age –
124

– 8 An Alternative –
154

– Notes –
168

– Preface –

I've always loved nonsense dressed up as scholarship. During my A-level studies in early modern history, one of my teachers gave me a copy of *The Holy Blood and the Holy Grail* to read and report back on to the class.[1] I loved it. Its *outré* thesis – that Jesus survived the crucifixion and went to live in the South of France and spawned a secret society, the 'Priory of Zion', that has acted as a hidden hand in the history of Western civilisation – was thrillingly written. And of course, as I took pleasure in pointing out in my class presentation, it was no less improbable than the Christian story of crucifixion and resurrection.

I cannot say that my teacher's point-by-point dismantling of the book's thesis was a shock to me; I never seriously believed its claims. But the debunking was disillusioning because my first exposure to the world of alternative history was so much *fun*. I felt the same about other works I devoured as a teenager, such as Erich von Däniken's *Chariots of The Gods*, a 1970s bestseller arguing that aliens visited earth and inspired the glories of ancient civilisations.[2] Books like these seemed to me to be delightful in their portentous ludicrousness. Finding evidence that debunked their

— DENIAL —

claims felt like a duty; it also felt like a disappointment. Although I was never taken in, I almost envied those who were.

My Jewish upbringing meant that I had been conscious of the Holocaust from an early age. As a teen who liked to read radical anti-fascist publications such as *Searchlight*, I also heard about Holocaust denial, although I never encountered it first-hand. This was pre-Internet, and it took commitment to track down such works – commitment that, as a soft suburban Jew, I didn't have. But I did yearn to explore this demi-monde. What could be sillier than arguing the Holocaust never happened? It was all a big joke to me. A Jewish university friend and I used to fantasise about forming a Jewish metal band that espoused Holocaust denial and boasted that we really do kill Christian kids and use their blood in our Passover rituals. On holiday in Egypt, another Jewish friend and I visited bookstores to ask if they stocked *Did Six Million Really Die?* and *The Protocols of the Elders of Zion*. What larks!

Today, it's harder for me to see the fun in all this. The breezy insouciance with which I consumed 'alternative' scholarship was based on the assumption that none of it really mattered. In my cynical, self-absorbed late teens and twenties during the smug 1990s there was no reason to think that neo-Nazis were anything other than marginal idiots; alternate histories and conspiracy theories similarly appeared to pose no threat to anyone.

— *Preface* —

I should have looked harder. It wasn't just neo-Nazis and fringe cranks who were constructing alternative scholarship; big business and conservative politics were doing it too. Of course, I knew that there were those who denied nicotine was addictive, who tried to prove that environmental pollution wasn't happening or wasn't harmful. I was appalled at this, but it wasn't my major worry. What I didn't spot was either their long-term determination to prevail or the threads that tied them to the shady world that I refused to take seriously.

Mea culpa. We are a long way from the smug certainties of 1990s liberalism, and my attitude to those who challenge real scholarship is no longer one of indulgence. As I will show in this book, for decades, centuries even, something deeply poisonous has been growing. This poisonous process has produced diseased fruit in our 'post-truth' age.

My focus is on denial and denialism, which deploy a cluster of techniques that enable those with unspeakable desires to pursue them covertly. What I thought were simply ridiculous (if sometimes nasty) examples of human loopiness, are much more than that. Holocaust denial is not just eccentricity; it is an attempt to legitimate genocide through covert means. Denials of the harmfulness of tobacco, of the existence of global warming, and other denialisms, are, similarly, projects to legitimate the unspeakable.

Yet I have retained just enough of my youthful indulgence that my approach to denial and denialism

— DENIAL —

in this book is not only one of condemnation. I continue to have just enough enjoyment of alternative scholarship that I can sense something more in it than just evil pseudo-science. I can feel the audacity, the joys, the predicaments, the wretchedness and – above all – the *desire* that courses through multiple assaults on knowledge.

That lingering empathy means that I have no choice but to recognise the allure of denialism and to face up to the fact that to condemn is not enough. How can one suppress desires so strong? Rather, we have to consider what alternatives are available to the deniers. As this book will show, these are neither easy nor pleasant. They force us to confront brutal dilemmas and hard choices.

I don't know whether confronting what I call in this book the denier's alternative can lead to a better way of dealing with our desires. What I do know is that, as I suggest in the final two chapters, we may soon be forced to do so. Something is shifting, something profound. And perhaps, in an odd way, cultivating an appreciation of the mischievous freedom at work in alternative forms of knowledge that I revelled in during my youth might be a better way of facing the dark times ahead than angry pessimism.

—

This book has been gestating for some time. I owe its existence to my editor, George Miller, who first saw potential in the project. I also owe a lot to those with whom I have discussed my ideas as they developed over the intervening decade.

More broadly, I owe more than I can express to my wife and children. Having a loving and settled family life has given me both the motivation and the peace of mind I needed to expand my writing and thinking in new directions.

1

– The Failure –

A chameleon changes its colouring to hide among the leaf litter. A cat flattens its shape and creeps soundlessly in the long grass. They do not announce to their prey that they are hungry and wish to kill to sate their desire.

Human life also requires that we suppress open expressions of desire. The range of circumstances in which this suppression is necessary may be greater than for other forms of life – hiding signs of sexual arousal, hiding envy, hiding dislike – but the principle remains the same: if we desire things, we may have to dissemble in order to gratify that desire or simply in order to be able to continue living alongside others.

Humans treat some desires as illegitimate. Further, humans generate a vastly more complex and diverse range of desires than non-humans, and they are enmeshed in a vaster range of circumstances. That leads to a similarly wide variety of ways of suppressing signs of desire.

How do we do this? Through *language*.

Human language allows us to speak not just of concrete needs, but also of abstract ideals. Language allows us to cooperate in small groups and to conduct projects that coordinate the lives of billions. The language we use is unique to us as individuals and at the same time a collective accomplishment.

Language is used to conceal as much to reveal. From the most sophisticated diplomatic language to the baldest lie, humans find ways to deceive. Deceptions are not necessarily malign; at some level they are vital if humans are to live together with civility. As Richard Sennett has argued: 'In practising social civility, you keep silent about things you know clearly but which you should not and do not say'.[1]

The same capacity of language that allows us to be social beings also allows us to shape how we understand ourselves and our desires. Just as we can suppress some aspects of ourselves in our self-presentation to others, so we can do the same to ourselves in acknowledging or not acknowledging what we desire.

When does deception become harmful? In this book, I want to explore one of its most pernicious forms. This book is about denialism, the danger it poses and what we can do about it.

Denialism is an expansion, an intensification, of denial. At root, denial and denialism are simply a subset of the many ways humans have developed to use language to deceive others and themselves. Denial can be as simple as refusing to accept that someone else is speaking truthfully. Denial can be as unfathomable as the multiple ways we avoid acknowledging our weaknesses and secret desires.

Denialism is more than just another manifestation of humdrum deceptions and self-deceptions. It represents the transformation of the everyday practice of denial into a new way of seeing the world and – most importantly to this book – a collective accomplishment. Denial is furtive and routine; denialism is combative and extraordinary. Denial hides from the truth; denialism builds a new and better truth.

In recent years, the term denialism has come to be applied to a strange field of 'scholarship'.[2] The scholars in this field engage in an audacious project: to hold back, against seemingly insurmountable odds, the findings of an avalanche of research. They argue that the Holocaust (and other genocides) never happened, that anthropogenic (caused by humans) climate change is a myth, that AIDS either does not exist or is unrelated to HIV, that evolution is a scientific impossibility, and that all manner of other scientific and historical orthodoxies must be rejected.

In some ways, denialism is a terrible term. No one calls themselves a 'denialist', and no one signs up to all forms of denialism. In fact, denialism is founded on the assertion that it is *not* denialism. In the wake of Freud (or at least the vulgarisation of Freud) no one wants to be accused of being 'in denial' and labelling people denial*ists* seems to compound the insult by implying that they have taken the private sickness of denial and turned it into public dogma.

Denialism and denial are closely linked. What

humans do on a large scale is rooted in what we do on a small scale. While everyday denial can be harmful, it is also just a mundane way for humans to respond to the incredibly difficult challenge of living in a social world in which people lie, make mistakes and have desires that cannot be openly acknowledged. Denialism is rooted in human tendencies that are neither freakish nor pathological.

All that said, there is no doubt that denialism is dangerous. In some cases, we can point to concrete examples of denialism causing actual harm. In South Africa, President Thabo Mbeki, in office between 1999 and 2008, was influenced by AIDS denialists, who deny the link between HIV and AIDS (or even HIV's existence) and cast doubt on the effectiveness of anti-retrovirals. His reluctance to implement national treatment programmes that made use of anti-retrovirals has been estimated to have cost the lives of 330,000 people.[3] On a smaller scale, in early 2017 the Somali-American community in Minnesota was struck by a childhood measles outbreak, as a direct result of the discredited theory that the MMR vaccine causes autism, persuading parents not to vaccinate their children.[4]

More commonly though, denialism's effects are less direct but more insidious. Global warming denialists have not managed to overturn the general scientific consensus that global warming caused by human activity. But what they have managed to do is provide support for those opposed to taking radical action to address this urgent problem. Achieving a global agreement that could underpin a transition to a post-carbon economy and slow the temperature increase was always going to be an enormous challenge. Global warming denialism has helped to make the challenge even harder by, for example, influencing the non-ratification of the Kyoto Protocol during the George W. Bush presidency and Donald Trump's stated intention to withdraw the US from the Paris Accord. There is no shortage of frightening predictions about what will happen if we do not act now to stall or reverse climate change.[5]

Denialism can also create an environment of hate and suspicion. Forms of genocide denialism are not just attempts to overthrow irrefutable historical facts, they are an assault on those who survive genocide and their descendants. The implacable denialism that has led the Turkish state to refuse to admit that the 1917 Armenian genocide occurred, is also an attack on today's Armenians, and by implication any other Turkish minority that would dare to raise troubling questions about the status of minorities in Turkey both today and in the past. Similarly, those who deny the Holocaust are not trying to disinterestedly 'correct' the historical record; they are, with varying degrees of subtlety, trying to show that Jews are pathological liars and fundamentally dangerous, as well as to rehabilitate the reputation of the Nazis. Holocaust denial gives succour to antisemites worldwide and has become an important part of opposition to Israel in some Muslim states.

The dangers that other forms of denialism pose may be less concrete, but they are no less serious. Denial of evolution, for example, does not have an immediately hateful payoff; rather it works to foster a distrust in science and research that feeds into other denialisms and undermines evidence-based policy-making. Even 'far-out fringe' denialisms, such as Flat Earth theories, while hard to take seriously, help to create an environment in which real scholarship and political attempts to engage with reality, break down in favour of all-encompassing suspicion.

The current controversy over the 'post-fact era', 'alternative facts' and 'fake news' did not come out of nowhere. Donald Trump, Alex Jones and Breitbart did not materialise from the ether. Rather, their prominence and success are the outcome of decades of hard work by denialists to encourage suspicion towards scholarship and science. In the post-war period, when the tobacco industry began its epic attempts to cast doubt on research that demonstrated the danger of their product, they were laying the groundwork for an even more ambitious project.[6]

Denialism has moved from the fringes to the centre of public discourse, helped in part by new technology. As information becomes freer to access online, as 'research' has been opened to anyone with a web browser, as previously marginal voices climb onto the online soapbox, so the opportunities for countering accepted truths multiply. No one can be entirely ostracised, marginalised and dismissed as a crank anymore.

The sheer profusion of voices, the plurality of opinions, the cacophony of the controversy, are enough to make anyone doubt what they should believe. Denialism's ability to cast doubt can ensnare any of us. The writer Will Storr, in his book on 'enemies of science', reflected on the corrosive impact of this doubt:

It is as if I have caught a glimpse of some grotesque delusion that I am stuck inside. It is disorientating. It is frightening . . . It is as if I am too angry, too weak to bear the challenge of it. And there is a fear there too, lying secretly among all the bluster: what if they're right?[7]

While certainty can be dangerous, so is unbounded scepticism. Denialism offers a dystopian vision of a world unmoored, in which nothing can be taken for granted and no one can be trusted. If you believe you are being constantly lied to, paradoxically you may be in danger of accepting the untruths of others. Denialism blends corrosive doubt with corrosive credulity.

It's perfectly understandable that denialism sparks anger and outrage, particularly in those who are directly challenged by it. If you are a Holocaust survivor, a historian, a climate scientist, a resident of a flood-plain, a geologist, an AIDS researcher or someone whose child caught a preventable disease from an unvaccinated child, it is obvious how denialism might feel like an assault on your life's work, your core beliefs or even your life.

Those whose life or work is challenged by denialism can and do fight back. This can even include, in some countries, laws against denialism, as in France's prohibition of Holocaust denial. Attempts to teach 'creation science' alongside evolution in US schools are fought with tenacity. Denialists are excluded from scholarly journals and academic conferences.

The most common response to denialism, though, is debunking. Just as denialists produce a large and ever-growing body of books, articles, websites, lectures and videos, so their detractors respond with a literature of their own. Denialist claims are refuted point by point, in a spiralling contest in which no argument – however ludicrous – is ever left unchallenged. Some debunkings are endlessly patient and civil, treating denialists and their claims seriously and even respectfully; others are angry and contemptuous.

Respectful debate and angry abuse, legal protest and marginalisation ... None of these strategies works, at least not completely.

Take the libel case that the Holocaust denier David Irving brought against Deborah Lipstadt in 1996. Irving's claim that accusing him of being a Holocaust denier and a falsifier of history was libellous were forensically demolished by Richard Evans and other eminent historians.[8] The judgement was devastating to Irving's reputation and unambiguous in its rejection of his claim to be a legitimate historian. The judgement bankrupted him, he was repudiated by the few remaining mainstream historians who had supported him, and in 2005 he was imprisoned in Austria for Holocaust denial.

But Irving today? He is still writing, still lecturing, albeit in a more covert fashion. He still makes similar claims and his defenders see him as a heroic figure who survived the attempts of the Jewish-led establishment to silence him. Nothing really changed. Holocaust denial is still around and its proponents find new followers. In legal and scholarly terms Deborah Lipstadt won, but she didn't beat Holocaust denial or even Irving in the long term.

There is a salutary lesson here: in democratic societies at least, denialism cannot be beaten legally, or by debunking, or through attempts to discredit its proponents. That's because for denialists, *the existence of denialism is triumph enough*. Central to denialism is an argument that 'the truth' has been suppressed by its enemies. To continue to exist is therefore a heroic act, a victory for the forces of truth. Of course, denialists might yearn for a more complete victory – when theories of anthropogenic climate change will be marginalised in academia and politics, when the story of how the Jews hoaxed the world will be in every history book – but, for now, every day that denialism persists is a good day. In fact, denialism can achieve more modest triumphs even without total victory: every day in which barrels of oil continue to be extracted and burned is a good day, every day a parent doesn't vaccinate their child is a good day, every day on which a teenager Googling the Holocaust finds out that some people think it never happened is a good day.

Conversely, denialism's opponents rarely have time on their side. As climate change rushes towards the point of no return, as Holocaust survivors die and can no longer give testimony, as once-vanquished diseases return, as the notion that there is 'doubt' on settled scholarship becomes unremarkable, so the task facing the debunkers becomes both more urgent and more difficult. It's understandable that panic can set in and that anger overwhelms some of those who battle against denialism. This can be counter-productive and lead to blindness and dogmatism.

One manifestation of this anger is the resurgent 'new atheism' that emerged in the wake of the 9/11 attacks, propounded by authors such as Richard Dawkins, Sam Harris and Christopher Hitchens.[9] For these figures, creationism is an outrageous symptom of the stupidity of religion. While outrage is often understandable, it often overwhelms the scholarly method that they are defending. Such scientists are often poor *social* scientists, finding it almost impossible to attribute creationism and other offences against science to anything other than religious idiocy and wilful stupidity.

One of the terms batted around in debates over religion, reason and denialism is 'enlightenment'. While this ostensibly refers back to the process, from the seventeeth century onwards, in which the notion of reason-based enquiry laid the groundwork for modern science, scholarship and the industrial revolution, it is too often reduced to a kind of buzzword, with limited historical meaning. This can prevent a reckoning with the more problematic features of enlightenment and modern science. As John Gray has shown, the Enlightenment also laid the groundwork for utopianism and apocalyptic thinking.[10] Modern fundamentalisms, religious and otherwise, cannot be disengaged from the rest of modernity – they are not simply throwbacks to a pre-enlightenment age.[11]

Denialism and related vices are also not the only threats to science and reason: governments and corporations that may sign up to the values of science and reason can, through secrecy, venality and cynical policy-making, undermine the free and open flow of knowledge. As Dan Hind has noted, 'the invocation of the Enlightenment decays into a kind of blackmail – "either you are with us, or you are against progress and reason".'[12]

Further, those who debunk denialism sometime come close to mirroring the denialists' conspiratorial and paranoid language.[13] There can be a disturbing similarity between the righteous posing of the lone heroic 'sceptic' who espouses denialism and the debunker who opposes him or her.

A better approach to denialism and other threats to science and scholarship, one I intend to pursue in this book, is one of self-criticism. The starting point is a frank question: *why did we fail?* Why have those of us who abhor denialism not succeeded in halting its onward march? And why have we as a species managed to turn our everyday capacity to deny into an organised attempt to undermine our collective ability to understand the world and change it for the better?

That inward-facing criticism needs to be carried out along with an outward-facing attempt to empathise with and understand denialists. Denialism is not stupidity, ignorance, mendacity, or psychological pathology. Nor is it the same as lying. Of course, denialists can be stupid, ignorant liars, but so can we all.

Nor is denialism simply a desperate attempt to avoid facing an incontrovertible moral truth. I do not believe that, if only I could find the key to 'make them understand', denialists would think just like me. A global warming denialist is not an environmentalist who cannot accept s/he is really an environmentalist, a Holocaust denier is not someone who cannot face the inescapable obligation to commemorate the Holocaust, an AIDS denialist is not an AIDS activist who won't acknowledge the necessity for Western medicine in combatting the disease, and so on. If denialists were to stop denying, we cannot assume that we would then have a shared moral foundation on which we could make progress as a species.

Denialism is not a barrier to acknowledging a common moral foundation, it is a barrier to acknowledging moral *differences*. The alternative to denialism is an uncomfortable – even frightening – prospect. In some respects, denialists may be more different to 'the rest of us' than we might like to recognise.

Nonetheless, while these differences may be profound, we are all human beings, cut from the same cloth. Even if I may have difficulty in putting myself in the position of people who believe profoundly different things to me, I can certainly empathise with the *predicament* that denialists find themselves in. Denialism arises from being in an impossible bind: holding to desires, values, ideologies and morals that cannot be openly spoken of. Denialists are 'trapped' in byzantine modes of argument because they have few other options to openly pursue their goals. While I myself am fortunate enough to have beliefs and values that I can speak about openly (if not, perhaps, in all social circles), I do know what it is like to have desires that I cannot publicly or privately acknowledge.

My approach to denialism recognises that denialists are never simply 'them'; they are always 'us' at some level too. My attempt to understand what the alternative to denialism might look like, represents a kind of shock therapy, an offer to denialists to imagine a different way of being. At the same time, that offer is shot through with the same ambivalence that accompanies any attempt to envision desire freed from its shackles.

I also recognise that my approach is likely to be seen as patronising by any denialist who picks up this book. No one wants to think of themselves as a denialist. Yet the issues I raise are universal. Denialist or not, most of us have been backed into a corner by our desires. And believe it or not, my attempts to empathise with denialists are genuine.

This book's centrepiece, presented in chapter six, will be a 'reconstruction', from found quotes, of the kind of arguments and language we might hear from denialists if they had the courage to abandon denialism and speak openly. This will not be pleasant or edifying to read, but it will, hopefully, demonstrate why denialism is necessary in the first place. By showing what the denier's alternative might look like, I am trying to address an absence I have found in other works on this subject.

This is not a book that focuses on debunking denialism's claims. There are plenty of works that have done that, with great skill and acuity. It is vital work – denialist claims cannot go unchallenged – but usually ineffective in winning over denialists. While I will, at points in this book, give evidence of the corrosive falsity of denialist claims, for the most part I will take this as read. Again, this strategy is unlikely to endear this book to denialists who are, for the most part, desperate

— *The Failure* —

to be acknowledged as equal partners in debate.

I am also agnostic on questions about the relative severity of different forms of denialisms, and on the moral character of denialists. While, for example, I argue that Holocaust denial and global warming denial – like most denialisms – share common features and techniques, I am not saying that global warming denialists are necessarily 'as bad as' Holocaust deniers. I do not think that all denialists are Nazis. While some denialists can be monstrous, most are regular people in an impossible situation. My agnosticism also extends to the question of whether denialists are liars. Some undoubtedly are, but sincerity is almost impossible to judge without the ability to peer into their souls.

In fact, in this book I deliberately avoid tackling the question of who denialists are, in terms of their life histories; I do not know what made them embrace denialism. There are multiple kinds of denialists: from those who are polymorphously sceptical of all established knowledge, to those who challenge one type of knowledge; from those who are actively contribute to the creation of denialist scholarship, to those who quietly consume it; from those who burn with certainty, to those who are privately sceptical about their scepticism. While I am most concerned in this book with those denialists who are active, public and convinced (the ones who, after all, influence the rest), what I do argue is that denialists share a *desire*. This desire, for something not to be true, is the driver of denialism.

2

– The Audacity of Denialism –

I have often been a denier. I have never been a denialist.

Of course I've been a denier. I have vices. Who doesn't? And where there is vice, there is usually denial. One of my principal vices is smoking. Like an alcoholic post-recovery, I will always be a smoker, however long I might abstain from inhaling burnt tobacco fumes.

I've never been in denial that smoking is disastrous for my health in the short and long term. I've also never found it difficult to give up; in fact I'm very good at it. My own weakness is starting smoking again – secretly – after periods of abstinence, sometimes lengthy ones. It always starts the same way: with an occasional cigarette at a time of stress or when out with friends. And I always kid myself that this time will be different and a stolen cigarette will only be a one-off, rather than the start of the road back to regular addiction. Then, before I know it, I am never without a pack of Marlboro Lights and a lighter, furtively sucking down the smoke whenever I can. Still, I continue to pretend to myself that I am not a 'real' smoker. I hide my relapse from family and friends, feeling a simultaneous thrill and crushing guilt at my habit. I try not to think where it is leading me. Then eventually someone close to me spots me smoking. In a paroxysm of self-loathing I renounce the addiction, until . . .

Isn't this bizarre? Here I am, publicly acknowledging a shameful source of self-loathing, honestly detailing the self-destructive process into which I have fallen many times, facing up to the fact that at times I delude myself in harmful ways – and yet I am not certain that this confession will prevent me from doing the same thing again.

This is denial at work. Not that I am in denial at the time of writing that I have an addiction problem, but that I have relapsed into denial on many occasions and continued to be in denial *even as I was aware of being in denial*. It is this simultaneous awareness and blindness that makes denial such a distinctive practice, and such a peculiar one. Denial is knowing and not knowing, acknowledgement and refusal, designed to protect something that is too difficult to directly address. It is not the truth, but not exactly a lie. It is sincere belief and cynical deceit. Sociologist Stanley Cohen defines denial as:

A statement about the world or the self (or about your knowledge of the world or yourself) which is neither literally true nor a lie intended to deceive others but allows for the strange possibility of simultaneously knowing and not-knowing. The existence of what is denied must be 'somehow' known, and statements expressing this denial must be 'somehow' believed.[1]

Denial might seem to be a very personal issue. Certainly, the popular use of 'in denial' suggests that it is a personal pathology that the individual needs to overcome by facing up to the reality of their problems. However, denial can never be divorced from the social world. I know this myself: my need to deny my smoking is tied up with the ways in which smoking is seen by others. If smoking had never been found to be harmful, if smoking was socially reinforced, why would I deny doing it?

Psychoanalysis shows how denial is simultaneously social and individual.[2] It is one of a range of defence mechanisms that protect the ego from conflict and the continuous assaults on it from the wider world, represented by the superego. Humans are driven by desires that have to be repressed into the unconscious id if we are to survive in a world where the full gratification of those desires is neither possible nor permitted. So denial is one of the ways in which we attempt to survive the constant friction between what we want and what we are allowed. Denial is also a way of protecting against pain and trauma, as when a child might escape from feelings of helplessness into comforting fantasies of power.

Denial is therefore 'normal' to a degree. In *The Psychopath Test*,[3] journalist Jon Ronson meets an

— *The Audacity of Denialism* —

ex-Haitian death-squad killer, Toto Constant, who appears to fit the profile of a psychopath. At one point, Constant breaks down in a fit of fake-crying, loudly proclaiming his innocence of the charges against him. He needs to deny in order to seem normal. Ronson also meets Al Dunlap, a disgraced fraudster and corporate downsizer, who blithely admits that his psychopathic traits are what it takes to be a successful business leader and shows no shame or guilt at the suffering he caused. Perhaps if he denied it, if he pretended to be a socially conscious businessman, he would have avoided disgrace and hidden his psychopathy.

As well as being normal, denial can even be strangely beautiful and even heroic. The 2017 film *The Disaster Artist* (based on the book of the same name[4]) portrays the filmmaker Tommy Wiseau's attempts to write, produce, direct and act in his self-funded movie *The Room*. Wiseau's film is usually seen as one of the worst ever made. His writing is incoherent, his incompetent direction results in multiple continuity errors, weirdly shot scenes and bizarre dialogue, his acting is an embarrassment. *The Room* is now a staple of the midnight movie circuit, and crowds turn up in droves to share in the mocking its atrociousness. And yet, as *The Disaster Artist* shows, Wiseau's stubborn commitment to following his dream, despite the lack of any conventional talent, is a monument to the persistence of his desire against all odds. Had he not been in denial, the world would have lost something that ultimately has given pleasure to thousands, albeit not the sort of pleasure that Wiseau had originally intended.

On a grander scale, denial can occur on a species-wide level too. Ernest Becker's well-known 1973 book *The Denial of Death* makes the argument that, given that humans are mortal but we build 'immortality projects' – civilisations, religions and other institutions – our attachment to these projects represents a denial of the fact of mortality.[5] Some have gone further to argue that denial is *the* distinctive human trait; one that can be dangerous at times but essential at others.[6] And if denial can be shared across humanity, it can certainly be shared across particular subsets of humanity, such as families, nations and even the psychoanalytic profession.[7]

Denial makes use of a panoply of techniques. It isn't just a simple refusal or a curt 'no'; it can involve elaborate rituals, institutions and processes. Denial is an active, social process, as the sociologist Eviatar Zerubavel explains:

Like silence, denial involves active avoidance. Rather than simply failing to notice something, it entails a deliberate effort to refrain from noticing it. Furthermore, it usually involves refusing to acknowledge the presence of things that actually beg for attention, thereby reminding us that conspiracies of silence revolve not around those largely unnoticeable matters we simply overlook but, on the contrary, around those highly conspicuous matters we deliberately try to avoid.[8]

When does this silence become dangerous? Kari Marie Norgaard's study of a small Norwegian town during the unprecedentedly warm winter of 2000–1 helps to illuminate some of the pernicious ways in which denial works.[9] The lack of snow, which meant skiing only became possible two months later than usual, boosted by artificial snow, was not just worrying from the point of view of the town's economy (partly dependent on winter sports), it also challenged the centrality of cold weather in Norwegian identity. The residents of the town interviewed by Norgaard did mostly acknowledge that the climate was changing, that it was the result of human activity and that it was going to cause them problems and changes in their way of life. Yet climate change never became an urgent concern in the town's political life, and its residents never fully acknowledged the seriousness of the situation. For Norgaard, this wasn't because people didn't care about what was happening – quite the reverse. Rather, the situation was too disturbing and involved too many difficult questions about personal sacrifices and duties to others, so it needed to be denied. She argues that:

Like the term apathy, the notion of being 'in denial' has a negative connotation – being incapable of comprehending something or behaving out of stupidity or ineptitude. I wish to clarify that a key point in labelling the phenomenon of no direct activity in response to climate change as denial is to highlight the fact that non-response is not a question of greed, inhumanity, or lack of intelligence. Indeed, if we see information on climate change as being too disturbing to be fully absorbed or integrated into daily life . . . this interpretation is the very opposite of the view that non-response stems from inhumanity or greed. Instead, denial can – and I believe should – be understood as testament to our human capacity for empathy, compassion, and an underlying sense of moral imperative to respond, even as we fail to do so.[10]

The value of Norgaard's perspective is that it shows how global warming denial – and, by extension, other forms of denial – might, in certain circumstances, be all but inevitable and certainly not a sign of malign political forces. However, when denial becomes official policy, it is harder to shift. Such is the case with the various forms of denial that retarded South Africa's ability to respond to the catastrophic impact of HIV/AIDS. As researchers have acknowledged, there was always going to be significant cultural resistance to implementing an effective response. In the era of white minority rule, AIDS was often dismissed as a 'black' problem and ascribed to their essential sexual promiscuity.[11] As the country transitioned to the post-apartheid era, other factors came into play, such as resistance to state intrusion into the private, sexual sphere. The end result was a cascade of official denials that, variously, minimised the problem, attributed it to stigmatised groups and to foreigners, and downplayed the necessity of treatment programmes.

Denial and denialism may be closely related, but they are not identical. I am happy to report that I am not a denialist about my smoking. If I were, I could track down research (or, more likely, cherry-pick quotes) that 'proved' that my inconsistent habit didn't technically constitute being a smoker. I could point to the fact that for most hours of the day I was not smoking and explain how my non-smoking time was more significant than my smoking. I could start a journal or even a research institute dedicated to showing that smoking was non-addictive. I could draw succour from denialist researchers who have 'proved' that smoking is non-harmful.

I haven't turned to denialism because I have no wish to turn my vice into a matter of public research, scholarship and debate. Whereas denial can be carried out privately or publicly, denialism is intrinsically a public matter. It is not just an attempt to prevent something disturbing intruding on one's security, it is an attempt to overturn something, to beat it back so that it no longer even needs to be denied. As Michael Specter, one of the most energetic debunkers of denialism, puts it:

We have all been in denial at some point in our lives; faced with truths too painful to accept, rejection often seems the only way to cope. Under those circumstances, facts, no matter how detailed or irrefutable, rarely make a difference. Denialism is denial writ large – when an entire segment of society, often struggling with the trauma of change, turns away from reality in favour of a more comfortable life.[12]

This 'turn away from reality' means that denialism is a much more ambitious project than denial. Denial, as an attempt to draw awareness and attention away from something unpalatable, is always vulnerable to challenge. It is a kind of high-wire act that can be unbalanced by forceful attempts to draw attention to what is being denied. My spells as a secret smoker in denial have usually been punctured by someone discovering me puffing on a crafty cigarette. This shocks me into confronting the vice, just as an alcoholic in denial might be shocked into rehab when friends and family stage an intervention.

Denialism is, in part, a response to the vulnerability of denial. To be in denial is to *know* at some level. To be a denialist is to never have to know at all. Denialism is a systematic attempt to prevent challenge and acknowledgement; to suggest that there is nothing to acknowledge. Denial is at least subject to the possibility of confrontation with reality. In contrast, denialism can rarely be undermined by appeals to face the truth.

All that said, denialism feeds off denial. Denial is the gateway drug. As Kari Marie Norgaard argues, global warming denialism leverages everyday denial:

The fact that nobody wants information about climate change to be true is a critical piece of the puzzle that also happens to fit perfectly with the agenda of those who generate scepticism. There is an important congruence between these troubling emotions and the psychological defenses they engender, on the one hand, and the social structural interests in minimising public responses to climate science, on the other.[13]

It is impossible to see an end to denial: it is too central to who we are as humans. But it is possible to imagine an end to denialism, precisely because it builds institutions that transcend the individual. After all, as we shall see in the next chapter, it didn't always exist. And while it is hard to find anyone who hasn't denied at some point in their life, few of us have been denialists.

One of the reasons why denialism remains a minority pursuit is that its sheer audacity requires a degree of commitment that can only be generated by intense determination and desire. Of course, that commitment and determination may vary between the pioneers of a form of denialism and their successors, as will it vary between those who produce and propagate denialist scholarship and those who merely consume it.

Where does this passion come from? Denialisms can usually be traced back to a kind of founding trauma, a shocking explosion of knowledge that directly threatens something fundamental to oneself or to a group of which one is a part. It is the intensity of this shock and the overwhelming nature of the knowledge that means that simple denial is not enough.

— DENIAL —

Imagine how it felt to be one of the following:

- An executive in a US tobacco firm on the morning of 11 January 1964, after the US Surgeon General published his report that unequivocally demonstrated that smoking dramatically increased mortality risks.
- A Christian minister reading Darwin's *On the Origin of Species* soon after its publication in November 1859.
- A Nazi supporter watching newsreels of liberated concentration camps just after the end of World War II.
- An executive for Exxon reading one of the many internal reports on the reality of climate change that it produced from 1977.[14]

In these moments, the future opens up into a number of possible paths. The main path leads where it should lead, where it has to lead to remain a decent person: towards accepting the conclusions that the evidence demands. Yet taking this path might mean sabotaging one's economic interests, repudiating one's life's work, or struggling to reconcile one's deepest beliefs with irrefutable contrary evidence.

The path towards denialism starts with a refusal to make such a difficult choice. Denialists are sometimes driven by greed or a desire to gratify their ego. They are sometimes liars or cynics. But there is no evidence

— *The Audacity of Denialism* —

to suggest that this is the dominant nature of denialists. In any case, all denialists share a burning desire to continue to appear decent while rejecting the path of decency. It is motivated by a yearning to carry on as one is, without conceding that one was ever on the wrong path.

So where to begin when confronted by such a stark challenge?

Initially, of course, the task might seem less daunting. The news still bears the patina of uncertainty. There is still time, there is still doubt, there is still hope. Yet this hope quickly fades into an awareness of a monumental challenge. Some, in fact, may flinch from it and retreat into sullen acknowledgement.

In a book published in 2014, the historian Bettina Stangneth unearthed a first-hand example of the wavering between denial, denialism and acknowledgement among those confronted with a terrible truth.[15] While in semi-secret exile in Argentina in the 1950s, Adolf Eichmann, one of the chief organisers of the Holocaust, was invited to explain what had happened to the Jews by a group of exiled Nazis and Nazi sympathisers, led by a Dutch Nazi collaborator and ex-SS member Willem Sassen. While, even then, there was considerable evidence of the horrors perpetrated in the Holocaust, Sassen and his circle hoped that the real truth had yet to come out: maybe the numbers killed were less than had been claimed, maybe Hitler had not known, maybe the Jews themselves were involved in a cynical attempt to gain sympathy. Sassen did not get what he wanted. Eichmann was too proud of what he had accomplished to collude with his audience's desire. Stangneth, having listened to recordings made in Sassen's living room, notes that:

> the researcher who is listening to these men conduct their investigations in Sassen's living room, and struggling through the transcript, notices that despite their will to deceive and to deny everything, they were unable to make any headway against the might of the facts. However hard they tried, they still heaped up number after number, even without meaning to.[16]

Perhaps because Eichmann's words and experiences could not be denied, Sassen ultimately did not fall into denial:

> Mass murder and gas chambers had happened, they were part of German history, and National Socialists like Eichmann had played a decisive role in creating them, out of their dedication to the cause. Sassen may have been a dedicated National Socialist and a racial anti-Semite, but he viewed this kind of murder project as a crime, and he was too self-aware to see denial as a solution.[17]

Sassen's mistake was to seek first-hand knowledge of the events he wished to deny. Most denialists do not make that mistake.

Effective denialism requires avoiding the quest

— *The Audacity of Denialism* —

for knowledge and making alliances. Denialists need to move swiftly, publicly and boldly. Naomi Oreskes and Erik Conway have described how the US tobacco industry mobilised against the mounting evidence of the harm caused by smoking that piled up in the post-war period.[18] They argue that the 'tobacco strategy', which focused on raising doubts about scientific research, is the prototype for subsequence denialisms such as global warming denialism (and some of the same people have been propagators of both). The strategy began even before the 1964 Surgeon General's report. In the early 1950s, evidence about the harm caused by smoking was becoming overwhelming. Oreskes and Conway argue that 'December 15, 1953, was a fateful day' as the presidents of the four largest US tobacco companies met in New York with John Hill, founder of the large PR firm Hill and Knowlton:

The four company presidents – as well as the CEOs of R. J. Reynolds and Brown and Williamson – had agreed to cooperate on a public relations program to defend their product. They would work together to convince the public that there was 'no sound scientific basis for the charges,' and that the recent reports were simply 'sensational accusations' made by publicity-seeking scientists hoping to attract more funds for their research. They would not sit idly by while their product was vilified; instead, they would create a Tobacco Industry Committee for Public Information to supply a 'positive' and 'entirely "pro-cigarette"' message to counter the anti-cigarette scientific one. As the US Department of Justice would later put it, they decided 'to deceive the American public about the health effects of smoking'.[19]

The campaign started to fund 'alternative' research to cast doubt on the scientific evidence, drawing on the work of contrarian scientists. By the time the Surgeon General's report was released in 1964, the research effort had begun to take centre stage:

Immediately, they redoubled their effort to challenge the science. They changed the name of the Tobacco Industry Research Council to the Council for Tobacco Research (losing the word 'industry' entirely), and severed their relations with Hill and Knowlton. They resolved that the new organisation would be wholly dedicated to health research, and not to 'industry technical or commercial studies.' They 'refined' the approval and review process for grants, intensifying their search for 'experts' who would affirm their views.[20]

Central to this effort was casting doubt. An often-quoted 1969 anonymous internal tobacco industry memo concisely summarised the strategy:

Doubt is our product, since it is the best means of competing with the 'body of fact' that exists in the minds of the general public . . . It is also the means of establishing a controversy.[21]

This approach to denialism was fundamentally reactive. It did not seek to build an alternative explanation for the persistent finding of a causal link between smoking and disease, because there was no way of doing so. Rather, it chipped away at the consensus by questioning particular facets of the research. By suggesting that the evidence was less overwhelming than it appeared, it sought to transform the consensus into a field marked by disagreement. The tobacco industry remained in the game as long as enough people – smokers and regulators in particular – could be convinced that the situation was not as settled as it seemed.

While the tobacco strategy demonstrated how denialism could forestall the sudden collapse of one's preferred truth, its weakness was that it didn't build for the long term. Although the strategy certainly meant that several decades of profits were shored up and new customers recruited, the war was ultimately lost and tobacco companies today rarely claim that smoking is not dangerous. The effort gradually switched to denying the harm caused by passive smoking and, when that effort too failed, to nurturing libertarian arguments against regulation. The industry is now faced with a different sort of disruption, from the increasing use of e-cigarettes, which they can adapt to using the venerable non-denialist tactic of switching manufacturing to a different product. The same pattern is likely to be visible with the fossil fuel industry. Denialism will ensure the continuation of the carbon-based economy longer than would have otherwise have been the case, but ultimately there is only a finite supply of their product.

The economic impetus towards denialism doesn't necessarily produce forms of denialism that are robust enough to withstand long-term challenges. When commercial circumstances shift, or when the struggle to be believed is lost, denialism becomes redundant. That is not good enough for those who are drawn to denialism when their long-term identity, beliefs and desires risk permanent destruction. They need to do better than temporarily keep controversy alive. For those who are committed to a vision of the world in which carbon-based capitalism reigns supreme, it is not enough to resist the fact of global warming for a transitional period until the argument is lost: in 200 years, their descendants still need to be able to show that untrammelled carbon-based capitalism did not lead to the catastrophe of the twenty-first century.

What may start out as a reflexive attempt to defend the indefensible often ends up generating a profoundly novel way of looking at the world. Parochial desires and interests generate revolutionary new paradigms with universal implications. When faced with insurmountable evidence, there is little other option but to change the rules of the game, to offer a perspective that, at a stroke, renders all the evidence suspect. Denialism becomes a new kind of scholarship, a new kind of science, even a new kind of epistemology. Not for nothing is Thomas Kuhn's seminal work *The Structure of Scientific Revolutions* often quoted in denialist circles: it argues that science proceeds in a series of new paradigms that emerge once the previous paradigm can no longer contain emerging findings.[22] Denialism seeks to be that new paradigm.

We must acknowledge the passion, the desire and the courage that motivates human beings to take on such monumental challenges. Denialism is a tribute to the ability of the human species to attempt tasks that seem impossible. So great is our confidence in our ability to reshape the world to our liking, that if the material world resists our efforts we will simply reshape our mental world.

The audaciousness of the denialist task can be intoxicating. The weight of opposition to denialism offers a challenge that is as voluptuous as it is intimidating. The tendency for denialists to become pariahs in many circles makes the heroic status that they achieve amongst their own kind all the sweeter. The prominent Holocaust denier Robert Faurisson rhapsodised about the 'revisionist' (the term most Holocaust deniers prefer to give themselves):

The Revisionist lives dangerously. Police, judges and journalists lurk in wait for him. He may end up in prison – or the hospital. He risks economic ruin for himself and his family. Little of that matters to him. He lives, he dreams, he imagines. He feels that he is free. It's not that he cherishes illusions about the impact of his findings. These frighten everyone; they are too much in contradiction to accepted knowledge.[23]

Even if the denialist might be marginalised at the present time, there is the tantalising possibility of subsequent (if possibly posthumous) validation. Faurisson again:

> the future will prove the Revisionists, as writers of history, were right. There is already too much evidence to show that the progress of Revisionism is inexorable. Revisionism is destined for a place in history as 'the great intellectual adventure of the end of the century'.

Yet however bold, denialism is also shot through with insecurity. While denialists may be proud to proclaim their research as cutting-edge scholarship, they rarely follow the implications of their work through to the end. It is only the most extreme denialists who challenge *all* existing paradigms and they rarely apply the methodologies they use to all areas of scholarship. How could they? That way, madness lies. One satirical website used denialist techniques to deny the existence of the moon, the Olympic Games and the *Titanic*.[24] In fact, denialists may be 'radical' in their chosen area, and utterly conventional in others. Denialists are forced into contradictory positions when the tools they use cannot be applied elsewhere. For example, as a global warming denialist, the British journalist Melanie Phillips makes much of the limitations of the predictive science of climate modelling and sees transitioning to a post-carbon economy as foolhardy

— *The Audacity of Denialism* —

given what she views as the uncertainty of the science. In contrast, in her continuing defence of the war in Iraq and her position generally on combatting Islamic terrorism, she advocates accepting a very high level of risk in military action.[25]

Denialism is, therefore, frequently as craven as it is bold. It is a revolutionary paradigm that cannot fully come to terms with the revolution it seeks. This is why denialist language is often an odd mix of swaggering insouciance and frustrated paranoia. Nowhere is this contradiction more visible than in denialism's attitude to science and scholarship more generally.

Denialism, and related phenomena, are often portrayed as a 'war on science'.[26] This is an understandable but profound misunderstanding. Certainly, denialism and other related forms of pseudo-scholarship do not follow mainstream scientific methodologies. Denialism does indeed represent a perversion of the scholarly method and the science it produces rests on profoundly erroneous assumptions, but denialism does all this *in the name of* science and scholarship. Denialism aims to replace one kind of science with another – it does not aim to replace science itself. In fact, denialism constitutes a tribute to the prestige of science and scholarship in the modern world. Denialists are desperate for the public validation that science affords.

Global warming denialists are among the most vociferous in claiming that they are motivated by a desire to defend science. The prominent US climate change denier Steven Milloy, for example, frames his work as a kind of crusade against 'junk science', which he describes as 'faulty scientific data and analysis used to advance special interests and hidden agendas'.[27] Melanie Phillips sees her global warming denialism as part of a wider campaign of resistance against the decline of reason and Enlightenment in the West:

The Enlightenment is consuming its own progeny. In the West, the culture of reason is dying, brought down by a loss of faith in progress and in the rationality that underpinned it. The replacement of objective truth by subjective experience has turned some strands of science into a branch of unreason, as evidence is hocked by ideology.[28]

While denialism has sometimes been seen as part of a postmodern assault on truth, the denialist is just as invested in notions of scientific objectivity as the most unreconstructed positivist.[29] Even those who are genuinely committed to alternatives to Western rationality and science, can wield denialist rhetoric that apes precisely the kind of scientism they despise. Anti-vaxxers, for example, sometimes seem to want to have their cake and eat it: to have their critique of Western medicine validated by Western medicine. That is why the now discredited doctor Andrew Wakefield, whose 1998 research paper claimed to establish a causal link between childhood vaccination and the development of autism, is such a hero to them: he appears to show that Western science can ground a critique of Western medicine.

The rhetoric of denialism and its critics can resemble each other in a kind of war to the death over who gets to wear the mantle of science. The term 'junk science' has been applied to global warming denialism as well as in defence of it.[30] Mainstream science can also be dogmatic and blind to its own limitations. If the accusation that global warming is an example of politicised ideology masked as science is met with indignant assertions as to the absolute objectivity of 'real' science, there is a risk of blinding oneself to uncomfortable questions regarding the subtle and not-so-subtle ways in which the idea of pure truth, untrammelled by human interests, is elusive. Human interests can rarely if ever be separated from the ways in which we observe the world. Indeed, sociologists of science have shown how modern ideas of disinterested scientific knowledge have disguised the inextricable links between knowledge and human interests.[31]

The sociologist Steve Fuller has gone further in suggesting that some critics of supposed attacks on science are not only guilty of authoritarian views on what proper science should consist of, they have a naive faith in scholarly systems such as peer review. For Fuller, supposedly non-scientific theories are identical in form to other kinds of science, if not in content. In the case of 'intelligent design' theory, he argues:

while intelligent design theory may appeal to those who believe in divine creation, its knowledge claims, and their evaluation, are couched in terms of laboratory experiments and probability theory that do not make any theistic references. Of course, this does not make the theory true but (so I believe) it does make it scientific.[32]

While I do not believe that the couching of denialist arguments in scientific language makes denialism identical to mainstream science, what both approaches share is an appeal to the authority of science as the pre-eminent method of legitimising arguments. This shared but competitive approach sometimes makes distinguishing denialist and non-denialist difficult.

In this competitive controversy, allies are crucial – or at least the appearance of having allies. Even though denialists may sometimes revel in their outsider status, if there is to be any chance of challenging or overturning the consensus, they need to show that they have support and legitimacy. Denialists therefore compete with mainstream scientists and scholars to build institutions that can endow their work with the patina of gravitas: think tanks, research centres, journals and conferences.

One example of this is the Institute for Historical Review (IHR), founded in the US in 1978 by David McCalden and Willis Carto, which has been an important source for the generation and dissemination of Holocaust denial, particularly through its publication the *Journal of Historical Review*. The name of the Institute is unimpeachably bland: 'Institute' evokes ivy-covered citadels of disinterested contemplation; 'Historical Review' allows the Institute to frame its work as part of a more general effort to advance historical scholarship. Its mission statement would not be out of place in many university research centres:

The Institute for Historical Review is an independent educational center and publisher that works to promote peace, understanding and justice through greater public awareness of the past, and especially socially-politically relevant aspects of modern history. We strive in particular to increase understanding of the causes, nature and consequences of war and conflict. We defend freedom of speech and freedom of historical inquiry.

We work to provide factual information and sound perspective on US foreign policy, World War Two, the Israel–Palestine conflict, war propaganda, Middle East history, the Jewish–Zionist role in cultural and political life, and much more.[33]

Where denialism defends a wealthy industry, the resources of that industry can be deployed to create a range of well-connected organisations and initiatives. Such is the case with global warming denialism which, like the tobacco industry before it, can count on the support of wealthy donors such as the Koch brothers and, in some cases, the oil industry. Institutions such as the Global Warming Policy Foundation in the UK, and the Cato Institute, the American Enterprise Institute and others in the US, are hives of activity. They generate books, pamphlets, conferences and videos as well as more surreptitious forms of lobbying. Such institutions have offices, employees and the money for international conferences and well-designed publications, all of which give the impression of substance and authority. In addition, global warming denialists constantly push to extend their reach with petitions, manifestos and jointly signed letters. Denialists are builders; they are innovators. This effervescent creativity is rarely appreciated by denialism's detractors.

The reflex reaction to denialism is, understandably, to show why it is wrong. The assumption that 'if people knew the facts' there would be no denialism is, unfortunately, often incorrect, as anyone who has tried to fight denialism knows. We are not living in a world in which knowledge is scarce: denialism exists in the face of a plurality of opportunities to 'know better'. Faith in the self-evident superiority of truth is misplaced. As Stanley Cohen argues (referring to the frequent failure of humanitarian appeals to spark action in the West):

Sophisticated technology can spread images of live atrocities around the world in minutes. But self-evident truth will not be self-evidently accepted. However informative, reliable and convincing they are, accounts of atrocities and suffering do little to undermine overt forms of denial. Humanitarian organisations are living relics of Enlightenment faith in the power of knowledge: if only people knew, they would act. Paradoxically, these same organisations know better than anyone how misplaced is a faith that they see undermined by their daily work.[34]

In fact, denialism can be rooted in an *excess* of knowledge. Knowledge can bring with it a responsibility to act, and, as such, to resist knowledge is to resist that burden. As Kari Marie Norgaard argues in the case of global warming:

The notion that people are not acting against global warming because they do not know about it reinforces a sense of their innocence in the face of these activities, thereby maintaining the invisibility of the power relations that are upheld by so-called apathy regarding global warming. Within this context, to 'not know' too much about climate change maintains the sense that if one did know, one would act more responsibly.[35]

Yet while denialism cannot always be attributed to ignorance – and cannot simply be addressed through transfusions of knowledge – it is also true that some individual denialists may be more knowledgeable than others. Social media has levelled the playing field; there are uncountable numbers of 'amateur' denialists tweeting 'arguments' that are unsophisticated or just plain stupid. There are complex obfuscatory arguments in favour of the existence of a flat earth, for example, but there are also innumerable tweeters who manage little better than pointing out that the earth doesn't look round if you look in front of you. Then there are the countless online 'activists' whose approach to denialism is little more than assertion, who shout loudly about the Holocaust being a lie without explaining why.

It is unwise to judge an argument by its least articulate proponents. To focus on denialism's knuckle-dragging tendencies is to confuse symptom with cause. It only takes a hardcore of committed, hard-working denialists to justify the gut feelings of many others that they are being lied to. Once robust denialist arguments are out there, they can circulate indefinitely, inspiring and motivating others who have no need to do the hard work that has already been done for them. That is largely the case with Holocaust denial in Iran: despite the sponsoring of high profile conferences and the official endorsement of some political leaders, Iran has added little actual scholarship to the canon; rather Iranian denialists repeat the arguments made decades ago by the likes of Robert Faurisson, David Irving and Fred Leuchter.

What then, does a 'good' denialist argument look like? What style of claims and proofs characterise the denialist canon? And how can you distinguish denialist scholarship from genuine scholarship? As the next chapter will show, it isn't easy . . .

3

– Doing Denialism –

One of the canonical texts of Holocaust denial is Fred Leuchter's report on his 'forensic examination' of the gas chambers at Auschwitz. Leuchter, an American execution technician, was commissioned to write the report by the prominent Holocaust deniers Ernst Zündel and Robert Faurisson, and it was first published in 1988.[1] The 'Leuchter report' was based on his examination of the remains of the gas chambers in Auschwitz, including taking (unauthorised) samples and submitting them for laboratory tests for gas residues. Leuchter concluded that what were claimed to be gas chambers could not have been used for the purposes of extermination, both on the grounds of design and a lack of expected levels of Zyklon B residue. His report provided apparently incontrovertible proof that the gas chambers were a hoax.

The Leuchter report is a sober document, suffused with technical details. Take the following:

Further, if the chamber were used thus (based on DEGESCH figures of 4 oz. or 0.25 lbs. per 100 cu. ft.), 30.4 oz. or 1.9 lbs. of Zyklon B gas (gross weight of Zyklon B is three times that of Zyklon B gas; all figures are for Zyklon B gas only) would be used each time for 16 hours at 41 degrees Fahrenheit (based on German government fumigation figures). Ventilation must take at least 20 hours and tests must be made to determine if the chamber is safe. It is doubtful whether the gas would clear in a week without an exhaust system. This clearly is contradictory of the chamber's alleged usage of several gassings per day.[2]

How is a non-expert on fumigation, poison gas and gas chamber design supposed to react to this? The claim made in the paragraph is clear enough – that a gas chamber of this design would take too long to ventilate after a gassing for it to be used for multiple exterminations per day – but is his reasoning correct? What do most of us know about how long it takes to clear a sealed execution chamber of a certain amount of Zyklon B, given a certain number of victims of a certain average size?

Leuchter's claim has, of course, been repeatedly debunked. The assertion that the gas chambers would take 20 hours to fumigate after a gassing can easily be refuted, as in this example by the online project Nizkor:

It is true that if one disinfects a building in ordinary commercial use, it should not be re-entered within 20 hours. That figure, however, has no meaning relative to the extermination chambers, which were forcibly ventilated. Fifteen minutes was ample time to replace the air after a gassing. When ventilation was not used, the Sonderkommando (prisoners used as forced labour) who removed the bodies wore gas masks . . . It is absurd to use the 20 hour figure in this context, as it does not assume forced ventilation and takes a huge safety factor into account. The SS didn't care much for the safety of the Sonderkommando who had to enter the gas chambers to take the corpses out in any event. In some cases, these people did suffer from the remaining gas . . . Furthermore, what makes ventilation difficult and lengthy is the presence of rugs, furniture, curtains, etc. Needless to say, these were not present in the gas chambers – there was just bare concrete, making ventilation very fast and efficient. If the '20 hours ventilation period' above was true, this would mean that the corpses of people executed using cyanide gas in US prisons would remain tied to the chair 20 hours after they were killed . . . clearly nonsense, as Fred Leuchter, who claims expertise in gas chamber operation, knows full well.[3]

Whom should one believe here? The Nizkor quote seems pretty devastating, but Leuchter's sober words resemble how genuine experts write. The uncomfortable truth is that deciding who to believe on issues that require expert knowledge is guided by factors extraneous to the evidence itself. One factor is how arguments are presented and for those who want to believe the Holocaust never happened, Leuchter's cool, technical writing might seem to be more convincing than the more accessible prose of Nizkor. The hard truth is that all denialists have to do is to produce something that *looks like* scholarship in order to be believed by those willing to believe. It doesn't really matter whether this simulacrum of scholarship has been debunked by experts in the field or not because, most of the time, experts are not the target readers.

Denialism therefore exploits a critical vulnerability in scholarly practice. In the post-Enlightenment world in which scholarly specialism has become more and more rarified, it is impossible to be a true polymath anymore. We have no choice but to rely on trust, and trust is earned by conforming to outward scholarly conventions as much as anything else. Even in fields where I am an expert, when I am asked to referee papers submitted to academic journals, I often have no choice but to take on trust what the author claims – how can I tell if interviews were ever carried out and, if they were, whether they are being quoted accurately? – and I am more likely to offer that trust if the author keeps to accepted standards of scholarly writing.

Denialism puts legitimate scholarship on the back foot. When debunkers draw on scholarly expertise to resist denialist claims, they can be forced into unwinnable positions. A detailed response to the scholarship of Fred Leuchter can position him as a legitimate 'other side' in a scholarly debate. This is why some opponents of denialism, such as Deborah Lipstadt, refuse to debate with denialists. But that, in turn, means they are taunted by denialists as arrogant or scared. When opponents of denialism respond with accessible prose, they risk looking unimpressive compared to denialists who revel in scholarly jargon. Take the 'Reality Drop' website, produced by the 'Climate Reality Project' to offer non-technical debunking of global warming denialist claims: it is a model of accessible communication of complex arguments, but in avoiding verbiage it doesn't flatter the non-expert in the way that denialism does; it lacks the thrill that denialism affords.[4] Yet when the situation is reversed and simple denialist arguments are countered by detailed scholarship, debunkers can look petty and obsessive.

To a degree then, denialism always wins. To present itself as a viable option, denialism can adopt scholarly or polemical styles according to what will work best with a target audience. Those who attempt to counter denialism can lose when they position themselves as scholarly experts and lose when they present themselves as clear communicators.

A 'good' denialist argument is, therefore, *any* denialist argument. Nonetheless, denialists still have to say *something*, they have to find ways to justify their alternative world-building. They cannot resort to standard scholarly methods, at least not entirely: they cannot respond to a mountain of evidence with a desire to be convinced, they cannot challenge their own prejudices and ask hard questions of themselves, they cannot build truly convincing explanations and theories. Their challenge is stark: they must find a way of explaining away the most likely interpretations of an overwhelming amount of data; they must explain how the data that has been gathered by most other scholars is unreliable or misleading; they must convince others that the implausible is not just plausible, but overwhelmingly likely.

In response to this challenge, over the last few decades, denialists have developed a range of alternative scholarly methods. Denialists cannot speak of them as they are simply presented as the scholarly method itself. But they have been identified and tracked by debunkers of denialism.

In 2006, a Holocaust researcher I know circulated a blog post he was working on called 'A Dictionary of Denier Fallacies'.[5] It consisted of a list of fallacious arguments that Holocaust deniers use. The list had 34 entries. Some of these were specific to Holocaust denial, such as: '33. Obsession with gas chambers/ Disinterest in Anything Else' (ignoring the fact that the Holocaust was perpetrated by a variety of means as well as gassing) and: '26. Jews Declare War / Hitler Didn't Declare War Back' (arguing that Jewish groups effectively declared war on Germany in the 1930s and Hitler was restrained in his reaction to this provocation). Some of them, however, were more general and could easily be used by denialists in other fields, for example: '6. Falsus in uno, falsus in omnibus' (one witness wrong, all must be wrong). The post demonstrated the sheer number of tools that denialists have at their disposal. It also demonstrated how denialism draws on tools that emerge from one field of 'expertise' as well as more generic tools from different denialisms.

There have been other attempts to create taxonomies of denialist techniques.[6] Some of these taxonomies are humorous and sarcastic, such as bingo sheets designed to amuse those who fight denialism.[7] As this book is not a debunker's handbook, I will not attempt a comprehensive list of denialist techniques. However, I will briefly outline three of the most common:

1 RADICAL DOUBT

What works with tobacco works with other denialisms. Almost any field of scholarship has its gaps in evidence, its ambiguities, and these can be exploited to open up what denialists present as irreparable fissures in the 'consensus'. It helps that many of the areas that are subjected to denialist techniques are inherently challenging to research. In the natural sciences, the linkage between cause and effect cannot always be directly observed. The process through which the burning of a barrel of oil results in a global rise in temperatures is not directly visible. The process through which smoking leads to cancer takes place over decades and unfolds differently between individuals. Conversely, the non-linkage between vaccination and autism is impossible to observe. In the realm of human activity, genocide and other atrocities are usually conducted secretly; the desire to conceal evidence to subsequent generations was woven into the fabric of the

Holocaust. The reason we know about these things is because of sustained scholarly effort to accumulate evidence from different sources within the context of a constantly evolving theory.

Despite the impossibility of providing 'incontrovertible' proofs, denialists demand them anyway. In 1980 the Institute for Historical Review offered a $50,000 reward for proof that the gas chambers existed. When a survivor of Auschwitz whose family had been gassed, Mel Mermelstein, offered his testimony, it was ignored and he successfully sued the Institute in response. In 2017 Junkscience.com offered a $500,000 reward 'to the first person to prove, in a scientific manner, that humans are causing harmful global warming'.[8] Robert Kennedy Jr. and Robert De Niro offered a $100,000 reward for anyone who could prove vaccines were safe for children and pregnant women.[9] Aside from the fact that such 'contests' are, by definition, unwinnable, they are also a mockery of how science and scholarship works. (Was Einstein motivated by a prize to 'prove Newton wrong'?) They deliberately misrepresent science as a search for absolute proof which, outside of pure mathematics perhaps, ignores the ways in which good scholarly work frames its conclusions as provisional – as the best conclusions possible at the time, given the methodologies, data and theories available.

The constantly changing state of scholarship is treated by denialists as a series of sordid efforts to 'change the story'. Global warming denialists have an awful lot to play with here: climate is very difficult to model and reconstructing evidence on climate in the past is equally tricky. As scientific techniques and empirical evidence accumulate, so predictions are revised. The same is true with historical scholarship on the Holocaust and other genocides, in which estimates of total deaths are constantly revised as new mass graves are found and new testimonies and documents unearthed. For those who wilfully misunderstand the scholarly method, such revisions are evidence of an inherent doubtfulness rather than constantly improved knowledge.

Disagreements between scholars are also misrepresented as proof of the weakness of the evidence. Holocaust scholars disagree over issues such as how and when the decision to murder the Jews was made and the culpability of ordinary Germans – but they don't disagree that the Holocaust happened. Climate scholars argue amongst themselves over how to model climate change and the relative importance of different forms of evidence – but they don't disagree that anthropogenic climate change is happening.

2 OBSESSION WITH DETAIL

Denialists also find opportunities in another aspect of scholarship, the profusion of detail. They focus microscopically on a highly limited selection of evidence and, by injecting doubt, they hope to show that if one part of the evidence is suspect, so the entire theory must be suspect. By baiting and switching, treating one piece of evidence as standing for the entirety, denialism gains traction.

One example of this is the popular denialist argument that there is no evidence of holes in the roof in the 'alleged' Auschwitz gas chambers through which Zyklon B was 'allegedly' poured. 'No holes, no Holocaust' goes the Holocaust denier's taunt. The Holocaust is reduced to arguments over the reliability of wartime aerial photographs of Auschwitz or drawings by survivors. Debunkers have almost no choice but to get sucked into this morass of nit-picking. It doesn't matter whether the nit-picking is credible or not; what matters is creating the impression that there are multiple uncertainties in one small element of the overall story.

All denialisms have their 'signature' details over which they obsess. For global warming denialists, it is the 'hockey stick graph', the Greenland glaciers and Canadian polar bear populations. For creationists, it is the complexity of the human eye. For anti-vaxxers, it is the presence of mercury in vaccines and the developmental records of autistic children. For 9/11 truthers, it is the inconsistencies and confusion in media reports of the attacks. Although denialism may exist in the service of grand designs and beautiful simplicities, its everyday practice is the very antithesis of big picture thinking.

3 CONSPIRATORIAL THINKING AND THE GALILEO FALLACY

Denialists have to face an obvious question: if what you are saying is true, why do most experts think differently? Their answer is usually not that most scholars have made an honest error, but something more sinister. For many denialisms, a belief in conspiracy is woven into their very fabric. Holocaust and other genocide denialisms are founded on a conviction that those who claim to be victims are actually the architects of a vast and devious fraud. The same goes for 9/11 truthers, who see the hand of conspiracy in the 'official' version of the attacks; and for anti-vaxxers, who see the pharmaceutical industry as cynical profiteers and the medical establishments as their bought-and-paid-for lackeys.

For other denialisms, conspiracy plays a subtler, but still essential, role. Global warming denialists talk darkly about the environmental lobby, but they have to restrain this tendency since the idea that environmentalists have more lobbying power than fossil fuel industries is a stretch even for the most committed conspiracy theorist. The failure to believe in the Enlightenment idea of progress, the pernicious power of the state and the erosion of confidence in capitalism are also treated as the causes of the global warming consensus. Similarly, creationists do not in general talk of self-interested lobbies and conspirators, but of more general trends such as the dangerous rise of secularism or even the influence of Satan.

At the same time, denialists also try to show that the consensus is not as complete as it seems. In fact, as they see it, were it not for oppressive attempts to censor and harass those who speak the truth, the consensus could even be overturned. As we have seen, denialists love to present themselves as heroic truth-seekers who struggle against the stultifying establishment. This 'Galileo Gambit' – which, aside from anything else, represents a logical fallacy as just because you are vilified, it doesn't mean you are correct – draws succour from denialism's stubborn marginality.[10] This is why the fact that denialist 'experts' are frequently non-specialists, is treated as a positive. While global warming denialists love to welcome the occasional maverick academic meteorologist into their ranks, or anti-vaxxers the occasional doctor, the fact that most specialists do not agree is simply proof of the corrupted nature of the field. At the same time, the accusation that denialists are conspiracy theorists or cranks is strongly resisted; one journal that published an academic study that found that global warming denialists were more likely to believe in conspiracy theories was eventually bullied into retracting the paper under threat of legal action.[11]

With these techniques and others, denialists have a lot to scope for building their alternate scholarly fields. But denial techniques cannot cohere into a method without an essential ingredient: a rampant and intoxicating freedom to create, to remake the world. Denialists give themselves the liberty to twist things, to misinterpret, even to lie or wilfully conceal the truth. The denialist can argue, as David Irving did in court, that the German word for extermination (*Ausrottung*) doesn't mean extermination. The denialist can argue that the epic poem *Beowulf* is proof that humans and dinosaurs coexisted as late as a millennium ago.[12] The denialist can dismiss the repeated premature deaths of people who stop taking HIV retrovirals as mere coincidence. The denialist can argue that the earth has 100,000 years' worth of oil reserves.[13]

Of course, some denialists use more 'out there' arguments than others, but all of them feed off each other in the great project of building a new world. Why would they want to give this world up? The stubbornness of denialism, the refusal to concede, is as much as anything a refusal to inhabit the stultifying world of slow-moving knowledge accumulation. Contemporary scholarship usually advances slowly and incrementally, with little scope any more for the earth-shattering breakthroughs that were made by the Galileos of old. Denialism is one of the few arenas left where the iconoclast can dream of upending the world.

And who doesn't dream of being Galileo? It isn't just denialists who fantasise about cutting the Gordian knot. In fact, it isn't just denialists who use denialist techniques. Anyone – from the most distinguished scholar to the lowliest tweeter – can fall into radical doubt, obsession with details, conspiratorial thinking and so on. It is perfectly possible to use denialist techniques in the defence of a consensus based on impeccable scholarship.

Denialists certainly have no qualms about pointing out when their opponents resort to dodgy arguments. For example, while any credible historian of the Holocaust will tell you that there is no evidence that the Nazis systematically used the bodies of Jews to make soap, the 'soap myth' has extraordinary staying power amongst Jews and others.[14] Denialists can and do point to the myth and say, 'See? If the Jews lie about this, what else are they lying about?' Denialists also made much of the 'climategate' emails leaked in 2009 from the University of East Anglia's Climate Research Unit.[15] They claimed that the emails showed researchers cherry-picking evidence and presenting it misleadingly in a dishonest attempt to prove anthropogenic climate change. Perhaps the best way to understand climategate is as a demonstration of the age-old tension between presenting data clearly but misleadingly and presenting it in all its opacity while failing to pick a path through it. Scholars constantly have to make difficult choices as to how to make an argument with complex and challenging data. They can, either knowingly or unknowingly, mislead and give an oversimplified picture of the world. In a field such as climate science, where scholars are constantly harried by denialists, the temptation to offer a devastatingly clear rebuttal can be overwhelming, even if it skirts around nuances and unknowns. All kinds of scholars can and do engage in 'immunisation strategies' against unwelcome information and defence mechanisms against challenges to the paradigm within which they are working.[16] Sometimes, this defensiveness can look a lot like denialism.

But there is a difference between denialists and their detractors even when they use similar techniques: denialists have no other option. Science and scholarship of the best kind are at least open to the possibility of revision. They can achieve robustness without cherry-picking evidence, without focusing on detail to the exclusion of all else, without setting up impossible standards of proof and resorting to conspiratorial thinking. You can make a good or bad argument to demonstrate anthropogenic global warming, the historical reality of the Holocaust or the reality of evolution; denialists can only make bad arguments against them. In this respect, denialism is defined by absence as much as presence. This is another reason why it is wise to judge arguments by their best proponents. If you search for the best argument for a position and find only denialist techniques, then you are looking at denialism.

There is another way of identifying denialism too; a way that allows even those of us who are not experts in a particular field to carry out their own debunking. Without really meaning to, denialisms make radical, even revolutionary claims about humanity – claims that denialists almost never openly articulate. Denialisms must stand or fall on whether these claims are valid.

Take Holocaust denial: for denialist claims to be true, there would have been two interconnecting elements of conspiracy. One element would have involved Jews and those they control planting and falsifying evidence during and after the war. This effort would have required coordination across the globe, within both capitalist and communist countries. The second element would involve the systematic migration of the millions of Jews who were not killed. Those Jews would have been removed to Palestine, the USSR and other countries, taking up enormous resources during a time of war, without any kind of publicity. These 'unkilled' Jews would never have spoken of this migration, nor would their descendants. Further, the countries hosting these migrants would have permanently excluded them from all future censuses and public documents, effectively requiring a dual system of state planning – with an official plan and a plan that includes the unkilled Jews and their descendants – that persists to this day. Not one official involved in this complex bureaucratic effort has ever spoken of this scheme. There have been no dissenters, or those that might have dissented have been permanently silenced before they could speak out.

The problem with this conspiracy is not just that

denialists have provided no convincing evidence for its existence, it is also that, if it were true, it would require a rethinking of much of what we understand about humanity. Are human beings really capable of such perfect, silent coordination of millions of people, speaking different languages, living in different societies across the globe, across generations? If so, it suggests that humans possess some kind of near-telepathic capacity that, as yet, no researcher has ever managed to identify. Indeed, so revolutionary would the discovery of this capacity be that denialists themselves do not claim that it exists.

While the need to account for masses of unkilled people means that Holocaust and other genocide denialists have made the most audacious claims about human capabilities, other denialisms also rely on claims that are nearly as bold. For global warming to be a hoax would involve, at the very least, the simultaneous scholarly failure of the vast majority of scientists worldwide, holding different political views, living in different societies and working in a wide range of highly specialised fields that are often incomprehensible to other scientists let alone outsiders.[17] At the most it would involve the active, secret coordination of most or all of them in a vast conspiracy. The same is true for scholarship on AIDS, vaccines and evolution, all of which have apparently become the consensus due to a vast collective, subliminal scholarly failure, or a similarly vast conspiracy, or a mixture of both.

Yet while such mass conspiracies are breathtaking in their complexity and in their ability to coordinate huge numbers of people without leaving a trace, they also reveal themselves in inexplicably obvious ways. For example, anti-vaxxers make much of the warning messages inside vaccine packages, which apparently constitute an open admission of the dangers of the product.[18] I once saw a video from a 9/11 'truther' that used official photos of the World Trade Center that apparently showed it was built without floors. Non-experts, with no specialist training, can apparently expose the life's work of highly trained scholars and a suffocating hidden global bureaucracy, simply by seeing clearly.

Conspiracies can and do exist. However, they tend to involve small numbers of people, to be limited in scope and frequently to be 'leaky'. They do not resemble the monumental and seamlessly efficient machines imagined by conspiracy theories.[19] Studies have suggested that conspiracies that involve anything other than a small group of people are simply unsustainable.[20] In fact, the central claims on which denialisms rest have rarely even been defended by denialists themselves. Rather, they understand conspiracies in much more mundane terms – as the upholding of a stultifying orthodoxy by covert or overt oppressive means. Denialists, particularly global warming denialists, sometimes draw the comparison with the domination of Soviet science by Trofim Lysenko and his followers from the 1920s to the early 1960s. Lysenko's ideas, which rejected the concept of the gene and natural selection, retarded Soviet progress in biology and agriculture for decades and resulted in the execution or imprisonment of scientists who did not toe the line.[21] But there is a major difference between the Stalinist domination of science in one country for a fixed period in time, and the supposed enforcement of global warming orthodoxy in multiple countries, with multiple political systems, among scientists from different disciplines holding different political beliefs.

Until some compelling evidence is offered to substantiate the claim that human beings are capable of vast, indefinite and silent coordination across time and space, we do not have to even consider it. In this sense, denialism debunks itself by resting on a proposition about humanity that denialists do not even advance.

Denialism also debunks itself by its persistent tendency to justify what it denies. While Holocaust deniers may not acknowledge the scale of the claims they are making about what human beings are generally capable of, they are less shy about implying that one sort of human being – Jews – are capable of these extraordinary feats of hidden organisation. This meshes nicely with notions of Jewish conspiracy and malevolence. If Jews really did manage to pull off a hoax so staggering as the Holocaust, and if it were only Jews that had the capacity to do this, then there would indeed be a strong case for genocide against them.

After all, how could the rest of humanity ever be safe if a subset of humans could deliberately manipulate so many people so effectively?

Holocaust deniers, together with other genocide denialists, therefore make the case for genocide through their denials. Usually this is only implicit in their arguments, but at times it can be explicit too. The American neo-Nazi James Mason was quoted as saying:

> It was indeed a damnable shame that Hitler did not, in fact, kill at least six million Jews during the war. We . . . know what the Jews were and are all about and we can shed no tears for any of them.[22]

Similarly, in 2016 one contributor to the far-right *Daily Stormer* argued:

> There is another important point that needs to be understood about the Holocaust story though, aside from it being a gigantic lie:
> Even if did happen, we as White people would have no reason whatsoever to be concerned about it.
> That's right – who cares?
> The Jews were the cause of World War II. They started it to crush the one European nation that chose to be the master of its own destiny free of the Jews' hostile, foreign influence.[23]

Denial has been described as the 'final stage' of genocide.[24] This isn't only a matter of preventing accountability and prosecution, it is also a delectable 'final insult' to the victims. By denying genocide took place, you attack the dignity of those who were killed even in death and treat those who mourn them with contempt. The taunt recorded by Simon Wiesenthal from an SS guard brims with anticipation at the prospect of post-war denial:

However this war may end, we have won the war against you. None of you will be left to bear witness, but even if someone were to survive, the world would not believe him. There will be perhaps suspicions, discussions, research by historians, but there will be no certainties, because we will destroy the evidence together with you. And even if some proof should remain and some of you survive, people will say that the events you describe are too monstrous to be believed – they will say they are the exaggerations of Allied propaganda and will believe us, who will deny everything, and not you.[25]

Denialists cannot avoid this slippage between denial and acknowledgement; their ideologies lead inescapably towards affirming precisely the thing they deny. Global warming denialists may deny that anthropogenic climate change is occurring, but if it was occurring and it was an urgent problem, the logic of their position would still be that it should not be addressed: the importance of extractive industries in free-market capitalism is so fundamental that we should at all costs maintain them, even if many will suffer for it. AIDS denialists may deny that HIV leads to AIDS and that anti-retrovirals are effective, but if all that was the case, there would still be reasons not to take these treatments: reducing our dependence on Western industrial medicine remains a key goal. Creation scientists may deny that evolution is a scientific fact, but even if it was, the biblical account would still be the true, even if only God knows why God-given science provides misleading information as to how he (for creation scientists it is usually a he) created the world.

Denialism therefore sits uncomfortably within a particular worldview. It represents a deliberate failure to follow through the logic of its arguments. So how did we get into this situation? How did ideology come to be so contorted? Why is it that desire cannot speak freely and openly?

4

– The Gap –

> In the towns of [the nations] which the Lord your God
> is giving you as a heritage, you shall not let a soul remain
> alive. No, you must proscribe them – the Hittites and the
> Amorites, the Canaanites and the Perizzites, the Hivites and
> the Jebusites – as the Lord your God has commanded you,
> lest they lead you into doing all the abhorrent things that
> they have done for their gods and you stand guilty before the
> Lord your God.
> – Deuteronomy 20: 16–18[1]

There's no sugar-coating it: this extract from the Bible constitutes a divine injunction to genocide. It is also utterly unremarkable for its time. Indeed, some scholars consider that the first mention of what became the Jewish people is in a proud (although obviously inaccurate in retrospect) celebration of genocide. The Merneptah Stele, built for Egyptian Pharaoh Merneptah around 1209 BCE proclaimed: 'Israel is laid waste, bare of seed.'[2] If you were an ancient emperor or warlord and had carried out a successful genocide then you could build a monument proclaiming your glorious deeds. The Romans were also not shy about genocide. Writing of himself in the third person in his

Gallic Wars, Julius Caesar frequently emphasised his genocidal actions:

He himself marched to depopulate the country of Ambiorix, whom he had terrified and forced to fly, but despaired of being able to reduce under his power; but he thought it most consistent with his honour to waste his country both of inhabitants, cattle, and buildings, so that from the abhorrence of his countrymen, if fortune suffered any to survive, he might be excluded from a return to his state for the calamities which he had brought on it.[3]

Such plain-speaking proclamations of genocide are not confined to the classical period. Early modern European colonialists would write books happily making the case for the extermination of subject peoples.[4] In pre-modern times, it was accepted that with war came the spoils of war – and that meant allowing troops (at least temporary) freedom to rape, steal and kill. Massacres and killing were commemorated and celebrated. Following the St Bartholemew's Day massacre of French Protestants in 1572, the delighted Pope Gregory XIII ordered *Te Deums* to be sung and commissioned commemorative frescoes.

Genocide could even be a pleasure for those who ordered it. Gengis Khan is attributed as saying:

The greatest happiness is to scatter your enemy, to drive him before you, to see his cities reduced to ashes, to see those who love him shrouded in tears, and to gather into your bosom his wives and daughters.[5]

Even as late as 1923, Stalin is said to have rhapsodised:

To choose one's victims, to prepare one's plans minutely, to slake an implacable vengeance, and then to go to bed – there is nothing sweeter in the world.[6]

But Stalin was speaking in private before his violent desires had achieved their full expression. There were no frescoes and monuments celebrating the massacres of the Great Terror. Earlier generations of despots had a language through which their bloodthirsty deeds could be proclaimed. They had much else too: systems of belief that legitimised and even sacralised the looting of wealth from their own and others' lands, the rampant inequalities that resulted from it, and systems of government, knowledge and social order based on faith rather than evidence.

And now? Now what could once be spoken of, even celebrated, is officially denied. It's not just genocide: the bad things that are done today by governments, by powerful corporations, by religions and other systems of belief can rarely be openly admitted, let alone justified. Today's denialists are the wretched descendants of the proud propagandists of the past.

In the last couple of hundred years, in the Western world at least, it has become much more difficult, even impossible, to openly and proudly justify some of the things that humans have been doing for thousands of years: exterminating groups of other humans; enriching themselves through making others destitute and enslaving them; destroying natural habitats; holding to practices and beliefs when they directly conflict with material evidence and so on.

What changed? On one level, nothing did. There is no reason to think that the basic raw material of humanity has altered significantly during recorded history (a minuscule amount of time evolutionarily speaking). Humans are wonderful and extraordinary, capable of incredible acts of compassion and amazing feats of invention. Humans are also cruel, greedy, selfish and violent. We are desiring beings. We eat, we drink, we consume, we shit, we fuck, we love, we hate, we labour, we sleep, we play, we laugh, we cry – and then we die. Our common humanity reaches down the centuries and across cultures. We can be moved by the dramas of Sophocles, we can laugh at fart jokes in Chaucer's *Canterbury Tales*, we can recoil at the patriarch Jacob stealing his brother's birthright. Anthropological accounts of pre-industrial societies brim with the same petty jealousies, joys and sorrows that we encounter in twenty-first century global cities.

None of that is to deny that there isn't still a chasm dividing human societies. I can't fathom what it would be like to live in a society where blood and treasure were spent on ensuring an Egyptian pharoah's passage to the afterlife. I can't empathise with families who kill their daughters in the name of 'honour'. And on the material level, writing these words after a recent filling, I can't understand how for most of human history (and still in parts of the world today), one might live with the agony of toothache.

Even if humans haven't fundamentally changed, the world they have built has changed dramatically in the last few hundred years. It's often called modernity: a complex of accelerating ideological and material changes that have transformed the world about us more rapidly and more fundamentally than at any time in human history. Sometimes building on, sometimes departing from the slow-moving innovations of our ancestors, we moderns have created the tools for the dramatic alleviation of pain, hunger and many other maladies. We have revolutionised our understanding of our bodies, the physical world and the social world. We have built upon existing institutions such as the state and the courts to develop institutions that alleviate the harshness of existence: the welfare state, democratic elections, universal suffrage, human rights legislation, progressive taxation, paid holidays, paid maternity leave and much more. We have attempted, sometimes successfully, to corral our warlike tendencies through the Geneva Convention, the Red Cross, the United Nations and manifold international agreements. We have condemned a whole range of once-normal practices such as tax farming and political patron-client relationships as 'corruption'.

As I write this on my MacBook, in my friendly local café on a pleasant summer day, with my tooth able to bear a freshly ground iced coffee, it would be ridiculous not to conclude that life is better today than it was for my grandparents and their ancestors. And yes, I am, in global terms, privileged, but in terms of my own country I'm not *that* privileged. Perhaps when Steven Pinker wrote *The Better Angels of Our Nature* and *Enlightenment Now*, in which he argued that, in some respects at least, humans have never had it so good,[7] he was also sitting in his local café on a nice day with a post-toothache iced drink. In these 2011 and 2018 books he argues that we are living in the least violent era in human history, not because humans have changed, but because of the historical forces we have set in train and the practices we have institutionalised, including the nation state, reason-based enquiry and global commerce.

Not so fast: even if it is true that the material conditions of human existence have improved for some, that is no comfort to those who still live in destitution. Certainly, the exhausted Chinese workers who assembled my MacBook and the underpaid Columbian peasant who picked my coffee beans wouldn't necessarily conclude that we are living in a much-improved world. In any case, even if the world as a whole is a less violent place, that is no comfort to victims of recent genocides and atrocities in Syria, Darfur and Burma. In any case, as Pinker acknowledges, there are no guarantees for the future. Global warming and its knock-on effects threaten to upend any notion that we have progressed as a species.

And even if you do accept that we have progressed, this doesn't account for the intense frustrations that this progress can bring. Humans may now have the knowledge with which to alter many of the fundamentals of existence, but this doesn't necessarily mean that we are in control of the process. While we may have more power to change the world than ever before, we are also more constrained than ever. This constraint isn't necessarily material – after all, we could end all human life through nuclear war, we could harness human creativity to colonise space – rather, it takes the form of a terrible psychological burden.

The burden is one of knowledge. We know more about our past, our future and the material world we live in than ever before. We can no longer hide from certain realities: that actions have consequences, that humans have lived in many different ways, that not all deeply held beliefs can survive scrutiny, and that in the long run people, ideas, civilisations, planets must die. We cannot hide ourselves from scrutiny; we cannot be sure that implicitly accepted beliefs and practices will not be exposed and made explicit. We may do the same destructive things we always did, but now it is almost impossible not to be aware that there will be *consequences* to our actions and that there are always *choices*.

Take ecological self-destruction. Humans have, on many occasions, damaged their own environment to the extent of endangering their own existence. Easter Island provides an often-quoted parable here: rampant deforestation, possibly exacerbated by the felling of the timber used in moving the immense stone heads, meant that by the time Europeans encountered the island in the eighteenth century, the population had dropped to 2–3,000 impoverished residents from as many as five times that number a few centuries before. Comparisons with the current exploitation of irreplaceable resources are hard to avoid. In his book *Collapse*, Jared Diamond explains:

I have often asked myself, 'What did the Easter Islander who cut down the last palm tree say while he was doing it?' Like modern loggers, did he shout 'Jobs, not trees!'? Or: 'Technology will solve our problems, never fear, we'll find a substitute for wood'? Or: 'We don't have proof that there aren't palms somewhere else on Easter, we need more research, your proposed ban on logging is premature and driven by fear-mongering'?[8]

Were the Easter Islanders really the spiritual ancestors of today's Amazonian loggers? The Easter Islanders inhabited a remote speck of land whose isolation was compounded by felling the only material from which a means of escape could be fashioned.

They may have had folk memories of the forested island that their ancestors inhabited and they may have regretted what had happened. Then again, they might not have done. Certainly, while the deforestation may have happened in a blink of an eye in planetary terms, it occurred over several generations in human terms. The Easter Islander who cut down the last tree had only known a land where trees, along with everything else, were a diminishing resource. The felling of the last tree is likely to have been a very mundane event.[9]

Today's Amazonian logger has no such excuse. Whatever his or her level of education, it is impossible for them to avoid the knowledge that, at the very least, many people regard the destruction as a crime and a disaster. The logger will know that unique species will be destroyed by their actions, as well as human habitats. The logging company will know much, much more and may indeed resort to the denial that Diamond imagines. Humans still do the same short-sighted things; they just can't avoid the burden of knowledge of the consequences.

A related burden is exposure. The ubiquity of media and academic scholarship means that it is impossible to be entirely sure that secret acts can remain secret. Certainly, even if it is possible to maintain a secret during a lifetime, there are too many examples of posthumous unmasking to ever be sure that, in the long-term, the secret sinner might not be consigned to the damned.

At the same time, while we are burdened with the awareness of the consequences of our actions and the ever-present risk of exposure, we have further constrained our freedom to act within a suffocating ideological, moral and political network. Somehow, in modernity the range and extent of what human actions can be justified has become more and more constricted. Gradually, the purest kinds of despotism, the most overt kinds of slavery, the starkest kinds of inequality have become unjustifiable.

How and why this happened is a topic for another book. Perhaps it might be possible to identify some of the stations on the way to our constricted modernity: the pieties of Christianity, medieval myths of chivalry, Enlightenment philosophy. But regardless of how it happened, we are living in an age in which any number of collective and individual desires can neither be publicly legitimated, nor practised without the risk of humiliating exposure. When Francis Fukuyama famously proclaimed in 1992 that the end of the cold war and the apparent triumph of liberal democracy constituted the 'end of history', he was wrong to the extent that liberal democracy now faces multiple challenges.[10] He was also right to a degree: this may not be the end of history, this may not even be the triumph of liberal democracy, but it is the triumph of paying lip-service to the ideals of liberal democracy.

Along with the other developments of modernity came a widening chasm between what is speakable

— *The Gap* —

and what is done; between what we are 'supposed' to be and what we long for; between the world we humans have built and the humans that we are. This is what I call 'the gap' – and it is the source from which denialism springs.

A gap has opened between private desires and the public language of values. This is a gap in language. Language is fundamentally public. Language both enables and constrains the ability of individuals to articulate their thoughts, needs and desires. Almost anything is privately thinkable, but many things are publicly unspeakable.

Of course, there is nothing new about a gap between public values and private desires. The very existence of a 'public sphere' presupposes a realm of civil virtue that is greater than the private realm of the individual. In fact, the very existence of publicly shared notions of 'the good' implies that not everyone can live up to it all the time. Only in a society without any kind of collective organisation and norms would it be possible for there to be no conflict between public and private.

Understandably, the complex relationship between collective and individual virtue has been a major preoccupation of philosophers and political scientists. One particularly taxing problem is hypocrisy: is it acceptable for human beings – and political leaders in particular – to publicly affirm certain virtues when they themselves do not always live up to them?

— DENIAL —

As David Runciman argues, hypocrisy is, to a degree, an inevitability; but what is dangerous is the notion that it is possible to live entirely without it.[11]

Nor is there anything new about justifying cruelty, greed and power by invoking higher values. Innumerable ancient and more recent despotisms justified enslavement and horrific inequality as divinely mandated. The tendency to justify power and the cruelties it brings is almost a historical constant.

The gap is disconcerting and uncomfortable; it has to be bridged somehow. There are countless methods of doing so, but I will briefly suggest five:

1 Accepting hypocrisy, in ways that might be cynical or simply apathetic.
2 Repressing and combatting one's private desires.
3 Making public discourse justify private desires.
4 Lying.
5 Developing techniques that cover up or deny the existence of the gap.

All these methods can be found historically and cross-culturally. However, I contend that today the gap is wider than it has ever been, at least in modern Western democratic societies, and that the fifth method has become more and more prominent as a consequence. We can see this in the history of European imperialism, which was – like most imperialisms – frequently accompanied by slaughter, greed and death. In response, defenders of imperial projects bridged the gap between bestial reality and the pieties of public discourse with increasingly sophisticated ideological justification for the exploitation and genocide of non-European peoples (the third method above). Yet the gap was only bridgeable in the first place because the violence of the reality was not itself denied, although it was rarely talked about and often sanitised for public consumption. The fact that the treatment of indigenous peoples in sixteenth-century Central and South America was publicly debated – with protagonists being for and against what amounted to genocide – is an indication that there was a much broader range of speakable possibilities available at the time.

Today, in an age in which the gap has become almost unmanageably wide, there is little alternative but to deny it exists. As a consequence, the techniques designed to hide the gap – denialism among them – have been elevated to an unprecedented level of sophistication.

This is not just an elite activity, confined to perpetrators of genocide and other crimes; it is part of everyday life for many of us. In affluent societies, there is no escaping the knowledge that distant others are suffering and that we are often implicated in that suffering, either through our inaction or as a direct consequence of our privilege. The psychologist and psychoanalyst Bruna Seu convened focus groups to look how this discomforting knowledge is dealt with in discussions of human rights.[12] What she found was a normative acceptance of the 'progressive humanitarianism' embodied in the Universal Declaration of Human Rights. Yet it did not necessarily mean that human rights principles were integrated into her respondents' everyday lives. Rather, the principles were affirmed in theory but their applicability was frequently denied in practice. The focus group members were often resentful at what they felt to be manipulative appeals by organisations such as Amnesty International and were quick to treat victims of abuse as somehow *implicated* in their suffering:

The vast majority of focus groups' time was taken up by discussions of causal explanations and accountability in human rights, and participants in all the groups spent a large amount of time debating why, and because of whom, atrocities were committed. While perpetrators were discussed at length, very little was said about the victims of atrocities. Indeed, very often in the focus groups I was left wondering who the sufferer/victim was, as frequently participants positioned themselves as the sufferer and as potential victims of manipulation, exploitation and shock tactics (see e.g. the 'shoot the messenger' repertoire).[13]

The language of progressive humanitarianism is often confused with progressive humanitarianism itself. Michel Foucault's major insight on crime and punishment is that, while we may have done away with the savage public violence of pre-modern punishment, we have replaced it with a violence that is more all-encompassing yet also more secretive, cloaked in discourses of care and the common good.[14] Modernity has seen the emergence of a whole host of institutions and practices, often of labyrinthine complexity, that maintain the ability of humans to inflict suffering on others in ways that are consistent with the requirement to be good, rational and reasonable.

We do what we always did, but in more convoluted ways.

Slavery is a test case here. We can see in the system of serfdom – which survived until the nineteenth century in Russia – a way of enabling a form of slavery in all but name. Once even serfdom was extinct in Europe, it was perpetuated on non-European peoples by developing new forms of thinking that consigned non-European slaves to non-human or quasi-human status. The Jim Crow system in some southern US states was another way of ensuring that, once slavery has been abolished, the racial hierarchies on which it relied could be maintained. Today, the *Kalafa* system in some Arab states ensures the perpetuation of quasi-slavery under the guise of monitoring migrant labour. Bonded labour in India is another example of slavery-that-is-not-slavery, maintained through the myth of the paternalist boss 'caring' for his childlike workers.[15]

Such obfuscations have been replicated in a host of other areas. The rise of 'public–private partnerships' and outsourcing of government functions to private enterprises are touted as ways of bringing greater efficiency to public works. They also provide a way of transferring public wealth into private hands in societies where outright bribery is frowned upon. In Israel/Palestine the extraordinary complex status of the Palestinian territories enables a form of occupation which is not occupation, separation that is not separation. There are multiple countries in which the outward appearance of democracy is maintained in public but made irrelevant in practice (even North Korea holds elections). In an age in which the concept of empire has lost legitimacy, the complex forms of economic, military and political domination by the superpowers of weaker states, have the outward appearance of scrupulous respect for sovereignty.

Denialism is part of this wider system of bridging the gap. As genocide became unspeakable, genocide denialism was born. As ecological destruction became unspeakable, global warming denialism emerged. As going against scientific evidence became unspeakable, so evolution denialism, vaccine denialism, AIDS denialism and others became necessary.

Denialism is not entirely novel. Humans have often held fast to erroneous ideas against a mountain of contrary evidence, using ever more convoluted arguments in the process. The conspiratorial element of denialist thinking also has a long pre-modern history: fantasies of Jews causing the Black Death, medieval antisemitic blood libels, paranoid fears of Catholic (or Protestant) conspiracies and so on.

Modern denialism differs in the greater necessity to deny, the difficulty of the task and the sheer range of techniques available to denialists. As the gap has grown, so have the opportunities for denialism. Bald assertion is no longer sufficient in political argument (although, as I will explain later, it may be making a comeback). Denial becomes denialism, an attempt to use the most prestigious discourse that modernity offers in order to remain in the right.

Denialism – particularly denialism in defence of greed and environmental destruction – is facilitated by the very structure of modern capitalist democracy. In pre-modern economic and political systems, there was no pretence that these systems were egalitarian; instead, pre-modern ideologies attempted to justify (and occasionally to criticise) this lack of equality, often drawing on religious doctrines. In contrast, modern capitalist democracies contain a contradiction between officially mandated political equality and the inherent inequality of capitalist economics. While this contradiction has been recognised to the extent that modern welfare states have successfully alleviated the more extreme forms of inequality, it is exceptionally difficult to recognise and justify the fact that capitalism requires that some people 'lose'. Even the most stalwart defenders of economic 'freedom' are reluctant to justify the suffering inherent in capitalism. For that reason, a vast ideological edifice has been built up over the last few centuries to justify capitalism without acknowledging its inevitable dark side. This long tradition of ideological obfuscation has formed the basis of many forms of denialism.

As the longed-for revolution failed to happen in advanced capitalist societies, twentieth-century Marxist theorists such as Antonio Gramsci and Theodor Adorno became increasingly preoccupied with the ways in which capitalism hides its true nature ideologically. The concept of 'hegemony' highlights the oppressive dominance of the subtle forms of ideology that keep the masses docile and unaware of their oppression and the possibility of change. Such theories can underestimate the degree to which social democracy can improve lives within the capitalist system, and they can also underestimate the degree of ideological diversity under capitalism, in democratic societies at least. Nonetheless, it is also clear that large numbers of people can be persuaded to oppose the very policies that could improve their lives. As Thomas Frank argued in *What's The Matter With Kansas?*, US conservative voters are often the ones who suffer the most from the policies they vote for.[16] Frank shows how conservatives are 'baited and switched' by right-wing politicians, towards socially conservative politics and away from any kind of recognition that their material circumstances could be better.

Global warming represents a stark challenge to

— *The Gap* —

engrained assumptions about capitalist modernity. As Bruno Latour has argued, we have never truly been 'modern', in that modernity was founded on a myth of the separation between humanity and 'nature'.[17] The modern man (*sic*) subdues, conquers and exploits the natural world. The idea that men could have, in their attempts to tame nature, unwittingly unleashed forces that threaten our very existence collides directly with capitalist modernity's foundational assumptions.

The Anthropocene, as the current age of carbon-fuelled global warming is becoming known, might, as Jason Moore has proposed, be more properly termed the 'capitalocene'.[18] Strong support for free market capitalism has been found to correlate with global warming denialism.[19] How could it be otherwise when capitalist modernity is based on a view of the world in which anthropogenic global warming, together with other unintended consequences of capitalism, are almost (literally) unthinkable?

Unsurprisingly, those who have a privileged position under capitalism are the most resistant to accepting the reality of anthropogenic global warming. White males are not only more susceptible to global warming denialism, they also perceive risk in general less strongly other groups – why would they when they have been the heroic actors in the story of modernity?[20] Global warming denialism has been described as 'regulation phobia'; a fear that the modern capitalist narrative of conquest will be damaged beyond repair.[21]

Denialism is also an outcome of straightforward material self-interest. It makes absolute sense for a tobacco, oil or pesticide company to use denialism against threats to their business. It also makes sense for oil companies to strategically plan for anthropogenic global warming, even while publicly denying it is happening.[22] Of course, it might also make sense in some circumstances for capitalist enterprises to acknowledge the harm they are doing, if that is what will ensure public acceptability and profitability. The point is that denialism is always a possibility as part of the range of marketing and publicity strategies. Nonetheless, it would be wrong to see denialism as always rational, even from a commercial perspective, any more than we should see capitalism as always rational. In 2016, a law was put forward in North Carolina to ban state and local agencies from basing their planning policies on projections of future sea level rises.[23] The law was supported by a coalition of local property developers. This may have helped their short-term interests, but was certainly not in their long-term interests. There is an excessiveness to denialism that, even when it is originally motivated by narrow self-interest, threatens to become mania.

For all denialism's excessive qualities, it thrives best in societies that are democratic, stable and liberal (both politically and economically). A 2014 study suggested that global warming denialism is strongest in Western democracies and stronger still in the English-speaking democracies that are 'freest' in speech and economics.[24] Not only do the most unfettered forms of capitalism nurture denialism, so does democracy itself. The connection between democracy and denialism is partly due to the simple fact that freedom of speech enables a vast range of discourses to emerge. It is also due to the constant need for democratic politicians to maintain electoral legitimacy. However monumental the mistake, what politician can ever simply say 'I screwed up'? However venal the motivation for entering government, what politician can ever simply say that they are in it for themselves?

Authoritarian states have less need for denialism as they can silence unwelcome information. When the 1937 USSR census showed that the population was not growing and flourishing as had been predicted under socialism, the Stalinist regime could suppress it and purge the demographers.[25] In China today, denialist explanations of the 1989 Tiananmen Square massacre exist, but are not the regime's principal tool for dealing with this threat to its legitimacy: the silence of censorship, the persecution of outspoken voices and the general preoccupation with capitalist accumulation over dredging up painful memories is enough.[26] Outside the country, the Chinese government has to work harder and that means sometimes resorting to denialism. One of the first denialist texts I encountered was a book called *What Really Happened in Tiananmen Square?* that I stumbled upon in 1991 in the Beijing Friendship

Store.[27] It offered a detailed riposte to the foreigners that the Chinese government could not silence, 'proving' that what 'really' happened in June 1989 was a just and humane response to a bloody insurrection.

Dictators may not tell the truth about themselves, but their lies tend to be more transparent than those of democratic denialists. Stalin's purges in the 1930s, for example, accused millions of people of conspiracies so vast and multi-layered that extraordinary proof would have been needed to make them even remotely believable – and, most of the time, proof was not forthcoming. Unlike later toilers at the coal-face of denialism, Stalin's prosecutors at the show trials had the luxury of being able to simply bombard the accused with assertions, that they then meekly assented to. Contemporary denialist claims are often no less risible, but they are cloaked with stubborn attempts at proof.

That said, denialists from developed capitalist democracies can be used to bolster denial in developing and non-democratic countries. Iran, for example, has imported and highlighted Western Holocaust denialists to boost the more reflexive forms of denial that predominate in the country. In South Africa, it was Western AIDS denialists who helped embolden Thabo Mbeki to build on the silence and denial already prevalent there. Yet we should not see this and other such cases as just Western 'perversion'. Rather, Western denialists provide additional fuel to pre-existing modes of denial.

— *The Gap* —

In some respects, a flourishing denialist community is actually a sign of a healthy democracy. Denialists learn their craft from the institutions that form the pillars of liberal democracy. The rule of law, for example, offers a powerful model of what denialism can achieve. A free and fair justice system is predicated on either defence or prosecutor offering an argument that is largely false. Denialist techniques abound in the creative search to affirm or deny guilt. Even the revolutionary impact of DNA testing, which appeared to offer the potential to conclusively establish undeniable guilt or innocence, has been countered by ever-more elaborate ways of denying evidence. One extraordinary example is the case of Juan Riviera, convicted in Illinois in 1992 for the rape and murder of an eleven-year-old girl.[28] Even when subsequent DNA testing found that the semen recovered from the girl was not Riviera's, prosecutors still managed to argue that he was guilty, by asserting that the man who deposited the semen was not the killer, but someone who had had earlier consensual sex with her (Riviera was eventually released in 2011 after three trials).

Denialism is therefore a symptom of the secret vulnerabilities of Western capitalist democracy. Free societies are not just free to produce dangerous and inaccurate discourses, they are almost compelled to do so. The danger that denialism poses is not that it will somehow reduce democracies to autocracies, nor that it will undermine 'Western civilisation' (whatever that might be). Its danger is rather that it will produce an ever more complete disconnect between the world as it is and the world as we wish it to be. This threatens to turn democracies not into non-democracies, but into a kind of shadow world where nothing is what it seems. While this shadow world is and will be full of impassioned angry debate, it is permeated with a stultifying consensus: no one is a cruel tyrant any more, no one is greedy, no one lusts for destruction and domination. Against this backdrop, politics becomes a kind of shadow play, in which – short of real discussions of real differences – all that is left is a battle over who can really claim the mantle of righteousness, who can rightly claim to embody the values we all sign up to.

Nowhere is this shadow play more prevalent than in the politics of racism. As David Theo Goldberg has argued, in a 'postracial' society, the very possibility of racism becomes erased and denied:

I assert my (non)racial, my postracial innocence not just by denying that I any longer, or ever, make (or made) racial reference or mobilised racist exclusion; I now further deny that I am in denial. I can't possibly be racist now because I never was then. My tolerance now – my openness to all otherness, or even more strongly to all my otherness – is evidence of my characteristic tolerance. So I couldn't have been racist then too. I can't be in denial because – tolerant then, as now – denial was never an issue. Thus postraciality reaches also for the denial of denial. I have turned my historical past into an empty white canvas, perhaps even a canvas of whiteness – or better yet a canvassing of whiteness. The postracial is nothing less than the vanishing point of race, and the supposedly fading pinprick of racism.[29]

For democratic societies to live up to the principles they claim to affirm, they would need to challenge and question the self-interest of dominant groups. Instead of going through this pain, it is simply much easier to deny one's racism. As one Dutch researcher put it:

Negative representations of the dominated group are essential in such a reproduction process. However, such attitudes and ideologies are inconsistent with dominant democratic and humanitarian norms and ideals. This means that the dominant group must protect itself, cognitively and discursively, against the damaging charge of intolerance and racism. Cognitive balance may be restored only by actually being or becoming anti-racist, by accepting minorities and immigrants as equals, or else by denying racism. It is this choice white groups in Europe and North America are facing. So far they have largely chosen the latter option.[30]

We are living in a world in which even the far right have signed up to the argument that genocide and even racism are bad – why else would the threat of 'white genocide' be such a preoccupation for white racists? The politics of antisemitism is similarly entangled in claims and counter-claims over who is 'really' antisemitic: among sections of the anti-racist, anti-Zionist left, the very possibility that they could be antisemitic – even accidentally – can only be a smear, made by Zionists in a cynical attempt to defend Israel.[31]

This kind of superficial consensus prevents genuine discussion of desires, values and morality. It assumes that there can only be one morality, one value system. This is a false assumption. I personally do not believe that genocide can ever be justified. But that's just me. The continuing presence of genocide in the world is evidence that others hold different views (even if, perhaps, others might only believe that genocide is warranted for one particular group). I cannot and must not assume that what I believe is what others believe. Yet in modernity it is almost impossible to know for sure where the differences lie, because we all claim to be the same.

Denialism exemplifies how in modernity we seem to have no choice but to affirm particular values regardless of how we feel about them. We are all of us caught up in this pretence to some extent – denialists most of all.

5

– Predicament and Pathos –

Can you be a good denialist? One of the problems of discussing denialism is that the phenomenon is so overshadowed by Holocaust denial. Given that the Nazis are widely seen as the epitome of evil, and that Holocaust deniers are seen as their apologists, all denialists can be tarred with the same brush. One can imagine how much this must hurt, for example, a Jewish global warming denialist such as Melanie Phillips. And while some denialists may delight in trolling and in the outrage they cause, for some the disgust they face must be hard to bear.

As I have argued, to suggest that denialists are despicable 'others' is to ignore denialism's deep roots in practices we all engage in. But more than that, denialism acts in the service of many political and social causes, not all of which are equally bad. While Thabo Mbeki's embrace of AIDS denialism may have caused real harm – perhaps more than any other denialism – among his complex motivations might have been ones that were, if not straightforwardly 'good', then certainly far from evil. Pieter Fourie and Melissa Meyer speculate that Mbeki was driven by a desire to escape the stigma of Africans as disease-ridden, sexually incontinent and incapable of governing themselves:

Maybe the reality of AIDS was such an insult to Mbeki's dream of an African Renaissance that he would do anything and believe anything in an effort to exculpate African culture or modes of behaviour – going so far as to question the science of AIDS itself.[1]

Similarly, the disgust at the sharp practices of big pharma and the medicalisation of every aspect of the human body that drives AIDS denialists and anti-vaxxers is not, in and of itself, a disgust that can only ever lead to bad consequences. Even global warming denialism is not generally driven by a desire for the suffering that global warming will cause: if they could pursue their cause without the prospect of millions of Bangladeshis being displaced, they would no doubt do so.

How, then, does one square the not-always-unspeakable outcomes that denialists desire with my argument that denialism is driven by the gap between what people desire and what is speakable? My answer is that it is the *consequences* of pursuing these desires that is unspeakable. A successful fight for inaction on global warming as part of a desire to preserve untrammelled carbon-based free market capitalism will inevitably cause the suffering of millions, if not billions. A successful fight against AIDS medication or vaccines as part of a desire to free mankind from the grip of

— *Predicament and Pathos* —

big pharma and the medicalisation of everyday life will inevitably lead to the death of untold numbers.

Denialism allows these visions to be pursued as if they were cost-free. Desire is preserved from the reality of its consequences. Even genocide denialism is driven by a similar fear of consequences. The Holocaust and other genocides inevitably involved dirty work – bodies that needed to be herded, killed and disposed of – that only appeals to a very small minority of even the most ideologically driven genocidaires. Denialism preserves genocide as a beautiful, spotless dream; as the cost-free removal of a hated class of persons from the world.

Denialism protects not just the unspeakable, but also the *unthinkable*. Some thoughts are too dangerous to be accommodated; inconvenient facts can bring down an entire mental structure. As we've seen, the psychoanalytic concept of denial helps us understand how essential mechanisms of self-protection, such as denial, are to the preservation of self. Yet some of the self-protection that denialists engage in is against facts that are simply inconvenient, rather than ones that could shake one's being to the core. One can understand why a creationist risks crisis if they accept evolution, or a free-marketeer if they accept anthropogenic climate change, but the stakes are less high in some forms of denialism.

We can see this in the case of denial of the Bosnian genocide.[2] It is totally understandable (while, of course, contemptible), that genocidaires such as

Ratko Mladić denied everything at their trials in The Hague, and it is similarly understandable that some of the Bosnian Serbs who benefited from ethnic cleansing will also deny everything. But less easy to forgive is the support for denialism from some sections of the Western left, or, more mildly, the equivocations from the likes of Noam Chomsky over whether the massacres constituted genocide. For such figures, the possibility that groups without Western support could do bad things is annoyingly inconvenient.[3] The same is true for anti-Islam campaigners such as Pamela Geller, for whom the idea of Muslims being victims is similarly inconvenient.[4] In these cases, acknowledging the truth might have shaken their ideological scaffolding, it wouldn't have toppled it. So why do it?

The same question arises in the cases of the occasional denialists for whom it is hard to see why they embraced denialism at all. The botanist David Bellamy had a long career as a broadcaster, scientist and environmental activist. Acknowledging anthropogenic climate change would seem to be an obvious step for him, yet he bafflingly embraced denialism despite the considerable cost to his reputation.[5]

What we can say in the cases of Bellamy and Geller and all those who turn to denialism even when there was no urgent need for them to do so, is that the desire burns as strong within them as it does within those for whom denialism is an existential life or death issue. Maybe it burns even stronger: why would you be prepared to accept the opprobrium which follows the embrace of denialism unless your yearnings were overpowering?

The personal reasons behind the desires that leads to denialism may be various, but what denialists do share is the common, collective effort to reshape the world as they would like it to appear. For that reason, the spectre haunting denialism is the disappointing, maybe even embarrassing, reality that we cannot mould the world as easily as we would like. Who has not had that sinking feeling when the realisation sets in that something for which we yearn cannot be obtained without sacrifices and unpleasant consequences? A degree of denial may be required to embark on any project whose outcome cannot be known.

Where denialism departs from delusions is in the degree of active resistance to the messiness of our desires. We are all stubborn to a degree, but denialists turn stubbornness into dogma. This can happen by degrees. After all, who starts off wanting to be a denialist? As Robert Park has shown, some forms of pseudo-science – one example being Joseph Newman's design of a motor that he claimed could generate infinite energy – start as simple mistakes:

What may begin as honest error . . . has a way of evolving through almost imperceptible steps from self-delusion to fraud. The line between foolishness and fraud is thin. Because it is not always easy to tell when that line is crossed.[6]

The obstinacy with which people can stick to disproved notions is attested to in the social sciences and neuroscience.[7] Human beings are not only reasoning beings who disinterestedly and rationally weigh evidence and arguments. Much of the time the processes through which we come to an opinion are pre- or unconscious, taking place in the deepest recesses of the brain. The search for evidence is as likely to be a search for facts that validate pre-existing views ('confirmation bias') as it is an unbiased weighing of the facts. As Jonathan Haidt argues:

The mind is divided, like a rider on an elephant, and the rider's job is to serve the elephant. The rider is our conscious reasoning – the stream of words and images of which we are fully aware. The elephant is the other 99 percent of mental processes – the ones that occur outside of awareness but that actually govern most of our behaviour.[8]

Scientific scholarship, even though it is a practice built by humans, meshes poorly with the adaptive strategies that make human civilisation possible. In this respect, denialism is a more 'natural' human behaviour than reason:

Our minds gravitate naturally to clear and simple explanations of things, especially when they are laced with emotional rhetoric. We are actually afraid of complexity. Our natural instinct is to try to get our arms around an issue quickly, not to 'obsess' or get caught in the weeds about it . . . this retreat from complexity is similar to the other reasons for science denial in that it is in many ways a useful and adaptive stance.[9]

It isn't just that the cognitive processes through which humans adopt certain beliefs may be impervious to inconvenient evidence; humans actively resist such evidence. The concept of 'cognitive dissonance' was born in the late 1950s when the American psychologist Leon Festinger and his colleagues attempted to understand why the members of a small apocalyptic cult not only failed to abandon their belief once the end of the world did not come to pass as predicted, they actually became more convinced and more active in their attempts to proselytise.[10] Festinger argued that the 'dissonance' between belief and reality is a form of psychological discomfort that is just as likely to be resolved by attempting to strengthen beliefs through a more selective attitude to reality than by abandoning such beliefs altogether. More recently, the strange ability for debunked arguments to resist counter-arguments has come to be known as the 'backfire effect'.[11]

Yet denialism is not just one more example of the ways human beings cling to discredited beliefs. One of the issues often left unresolved by psychology and neuroscience is why some sorts of beliefs are more resistant to correction than others. Think of a couple driving to a restaurant for dinner: one of them argues it is on the left-hand side of the street, the other that it is on the right. An argument ensues. It turns out that it is on the left. The 'right-hand' partner may make excuses about why s/he was mistaken and may accuse the other of being intolerant of their mistakes – but s/he is very unlikely to continue to insist that the restaurant is on the right. Why is it different when a global warming denialist is confronted with a mountain of evidence for anthropogenic climate change? Perhaps one's 'elephant' – which ultimately derives from entrenched moral convictions – rules over some issues (political ones in particular) but not others. Fair enough, but this doesn't account for the ways in which denialism acts as a moral masquerade, in which the true nature of these elephants is disguised. When a global warming denialist evinces concern for the impact on the developing world of any transition to a post-carbon economy, it is not a moral elephant that is in charge – it is a fantasy version of what they would like that elephant to be.

There is also a difference between the preconscious search for confirmation of existing views that we all engage in to some extent and the deliberate attempt to dress this search up as a quest for truth. An apocalyptic cult may attempt to reduce cognitive dissonance through means that they are barely aware of; denialists are engaged in a public proclamation of the disinterested nature of their attempts to do the same. Denialism therefore adds extra layers of reinforcement and defence around widely shared psychological practices with the (never articulated) aim of preventing their exposure. This certainly makes changing the minds of denialists even more difficult than changing the minds of the rest of stubborn humanity.

One crumb of comfort is that, in a few instances, the masquerade of disinterested scholarship may be clung onto so intensely that it can be transformed into more genuine open-mindedness. Genuine 'climate sceptics', for example, sometimes do come around, although this can be despite rather than because of the efforts of environmental campaigners. Michael Shermer, the US publisher of *Skeptic* magazine, who has been a prominent debunker of Holocaust denial and pseudoscience, explained in 2008 that the tardiness of his eventual acceptance of the reality of anthropogenic global warming was a result of 'getting burnt' by erroneous predictions made by environmentalists.[12] Another 'former sceptic', Berkeley University scientist Richard A. Muller, also criticised what he considered unprovable claims made by some environmentalists (for example, that the severity of Hurricane Katrina was directly linked to climate change) in a 2012 article explaining how an extensive study by him and colleagues finally convinced him of the reality of anthropogenic climate change.[13] In both cases, it was only uncoupling the science from its presumed political and moral implications that enabled the belated conversion. By trying to live up to the Enlightenment principle that science is ideally disconnected from politics, such sceptics were able to avoid falling permanently into denialism.

At the risk of searching for confirmation bias for my own argument, one might argue that such individuals were never really full-blown denialists in the first place: just people with unhelpfully high levels of scepticism seasoned with a truculent reluctance to go along with the majority. Given that these are exceptional cases, it may well be that evidence and counter-arguments do not work with most denialists, but perhaps something else will? Is any denialist really beyond 'saving'? My quasi-religious, quasi-medical (and fully patronising) use of the word 'saving' is deliberate, not because I consider denialists to be somehow fallen and corrupted, but because denialism is shot through with desperation and anxiety that shows it to be a kind of predicament; a burden, for all the bluster and defiance.

One of the consequences of the outrage that denialism provokes is that it can become difficult to see denialism as anything other than noxious and false. If one reads denialist works simply in order to debunk them, one can miss the pathos, the desperation and the fierce hope that undergirds them. Take the following section from a monologue by the infamous US radio host Rush Limbaugh:

I can't come to grips intellectually with the idea that the way we live our lives – and I don't have any doubt that the Western civilisation lifestyle provides the best opportunity, the best chance for humanity on this entire planet. And yet every day I'm pummeled with the charge, with the allegation that all of us who are simply trying to provide for ourselves and our families, we're trying to better our communities, we are trying to improve the future for our children, I just can't accept that the process of doing all of that leads to the destruction of all that has been created for us. I don't think we have the power.[14]

There is infuriating stubbornness here, there is dangerous blindness – and there is also poignancy. Limbaugh reveals the extent to which denialists can feel cornered, trapped, their hopes, dreams and fantasies under threat.

Under pressure to yield, such fantasies can even be turned into something almost beautiful. One strain in global warming denialism views the earth's 'resilience' with a kind of awe; anthropogenic climate change is impossible because our world is greater than we are.[15] This appreciation of the earth can be combined with a similar awe at human ingenuity at exploiting its bounty. One denialist has even called oil an 'infinite' resource, whose potential is limited only by human abilities to extract and make use of it.[16] Denialism thus reaches out to touch the face of God, invoking the wondrous limitlessness of existence. Against this joyful fantasy, what does acceptance of the fact of anthropogenic global warming offer other than deflation?

Denialism can therefore propose a kind of perverse wager: why not bet everything on the possibility that the world is infinitely amenable to what we would like it to be? As one anti-vaxxer puts it:

You must choose whether you believe that the body has an innate wisdom, a vitalism that guides its natively harmonious performance. That illness is evidence of imbalance somewhere – physically, mentally, spiritually, interpersonally, nutritionally – and that it is an invitation to engage change in the service of this balance. Or: Whether you believe that we are born with our destiny set by our genes. That our bodies are finely calibrated machines that are prone to break-down, requiring repair, servicing, and maintenance. That 'the science is settled' (about anything). That doctors are beyond reproach.[17]

Yet this defiance, this quasi-utopianism, can never entirely disengage itself from the threatening, creeping intrusion of miserable reality. Just as denialists in the tobacco and oil industries can only put off their day of reckoning for a while, so denialism as a whole is constantly fighting a battle with posterity. We know how history always identifies heroes and villains after the fact, and who wants to be a villain? Today's global warming denialists risk being cursed and ridiculed in the future. That is why it is almost an insult to ask if denialists 'really' mean what they say – who would risk future opprobrium, perhaps even within one's lifetime, if one wasn't absolutely committed to one's beliefs?

This outrageous risk-taking is driven as much by desperation as bravery. Holocaust denial and other forms of genocide denialism are haunted by the usually unpleasant fate of those who actually committed mass murder. During and after the war, Nazi genocidaires were left without any kind of language to justify their deeds. In Gitta Sereny's *Into That Darkness*, Franz Stangl, the commandant of Treblinka, is unmoored by her forensic questioning: he cannot justify the killings yet he cannot fully concede how deeply he was implicated in something that he could not deny was evil.[18] In a similarly excruciating meeting with the survivor Toivi Blatt in 1983, Sobibor Commandant Karl Frenzel alternates between half-hearted expressions of guilt and limp attempts to minimise his culpability.[19]

This bathos is not simply the result of the Nazis losing the war. In his infamous speech in Posen in 1943, which offers a rare recorded instance of a senior Nazi discussing the extermination of the Jews, Heinrich Himmler referred to the genocide as 'a page of glory never mentioned and never to be mentioned'.[20] There was a warning here: that those who carried out mass murder would never be publicly glorified for their deeds. If the Nazis had won, the likes of Stangl would never have had streets named after them. Rather, those who did the dirty work of genocide would have likely suffered the same fate as Vasily Blokhin in the Soviet Union: the NKVD killer personally executed 7,000 Poles in the Katyn massacre in 1940 and who knows how many of his own countrymen throughout his career. Yet he was never lauded as a hero. After Stalin's death, he was quickly stripped of his position and died in obscurity in 1955.

Genocide denialism doesn't just insult the victims

of genocide, it insults the perpetrators too. How could it be otherwise? Genocide denialists have few alternatives: if they wish to maintain the reputations of those who have conducted genocide in the past, together with the option of conducting it again in the future then they have no alternative but to effectively repudiate the actions of their those who should be their heroes. In doing so, they continue to perpetuate the furtiveness that has accompanied modern genocides and condemns their perpetrators to silence or ignominy.

Denialists are caught in a trap of their own making. In order to keep the flame of their desire alive, they have to turn their backs on real embodiments of that desire. They have to deny even that which their beliefs would seem to embrace. It is as though their desire fails them at the crucial point. Everything they argue seems to point to a certain end, yet they have to swerve away just before the moment of consummation. If the Jews are so pernicious, why not call for their extermination and praise previous attempts to do just that? If one believes so strongly in free market capitalism founded on the exploitation of scarce resources, then surely the costs of global warming are worth paying in blood? If one believes that industrialised medicine is so dehumanising, then surely the deaths of untold numbers of children is a small price to pay?

Denialism embodies desire then, but it is bathetic desire. A flat earther starts off with a vision of a gloriously simple world that is exactly what it looks like; a flat earther ends up constructing infernally complex models that explain just how a ship can 'appear' to sail in one direction and eventually end up exactly where it started. A global warming denialist starts off wanting to preserve the capitalist world as it is; a global warming denialist ends up taking part in endless disputes over polar bear populations in the Arctic.[21] A Holocaust denier starts off wanting to keep the idea of the infernal Jewish conspiracy alive; a Holocaust denier ends up trying to prove that Hitler was a magnanimous friend to the Jews.

And amidst these endless contortions the denialist suffers constant humiliations from adversaries who can always call on more and better evidence. Sure, a global warming denialist may enjoy well-funded think tank positions, but s/he will never ascend to the scholarly pantheon. Sure, David Irving may be lionised by followers at semi-secret meetings in the back rooms of country pubs, he may adopt the air of the persecuted intellectual but, unlike his trial nemesis Richard Evans, he will never be Cambridge University Regius Professor of History, and unlike Deborah Lipstadt he will never be immortalised as the hero of a Hollywood film.

Lonely is the denialist. No wonder the back cover of the edition of the Leuchter Report published by David Irving's Focal Point Publications features apparently supportive quotes by prominent writers on the Holocaust such as Hannah Arendt and Raul Hilberg:[22] even your enemy's fabricated support is better than no support at all. No wonder denialists almost plead to be debated with.

It's only the most belligerent of ideologists who have the strength to resist this heroic ignominy. In his book on neopagan and occultist forms of white supremacy, Matthias Gardell discussed the American Odinist Wyatt Kaldenberg, a rare example of a Jew-hater who despises Holocaust denial:

Believing that Jews act as principal agents of the demiurge, Kaldenberg spared no scorn for Holocaust deniers who tried to make Hitler into a Boy Scout who would not hurt his declared racial enemies. Only a mind weakened by reality-distorting Christianity would apologise for killing one's enemy, while a 'pagan view of the Holocaust' would be the very opposite. 'Human history is a chain of Holocausts. He who kills his opposition wins. Winning is what survival is all about.' Accusing the Jews of murdering 300 million European pagans during 2,000 years of Jewish Christianity, Kaldenberg felt the proper question Aryans should ask was rather 'why we didn't grease the Jews sooner?' The revisionist element in the racial movement proved to Kaldenberg that the sons of the sun had yet to awaken to their true mission. 'If we were real Aryans, we would not be denying that we defeated the Jews.' Places like 'Auschwitz and Dachau [should be turned] into religious shrines because evil died there,' he asserted, continuing that 'Holocaust Remembrance Day must become one of our holy days. We must remember the day when good defeated evil'.[23]

— *Predicament and Pathos* —

Kaldenberg is correct: there is a failure of will in Holocaust denial that ill befits the Aryan Übermensch. But as one might expect for an Odinist who believes in the power of individual sovereignty rather than in empathy, Kaldenberg cannot see the very real predicament that denialists are caught up in that impels them towards cutting the intoxicating drug of desire with self-subverting evasions.

—

Even if denialists are caught in a trap they may not even know exists, we still have to ask: is this absolutely inevitable? Denialism hasn't always existed, and maybe it doesn't have to exist in the future.

Any human practice not required for material survival, however engrained it might seem, involves a choice. To argue otherwise isn't just to give in to fatalism, it flies in the face of historical and anthropological evidence that humans behave and have behaved in diverse ways. Even if choice is constrained and difficult, every moment is pregnant with possibility. Denialists could act differently.

So far, so hopeful. And those who criticise and fight denialism must, at some level, share at least a morsel of this hope.

The problem is that the hope for change can itself be imbued with assumptions that reveal ways of thinking every bit as constrained as those of denialists. To oppose denialism is to hold out hope that denialists will come to accept certain facts. But too often, the hope goes further in assuming that the acceptance of science and scholarship will also lead to certain moral and political conclusions: Holocaust deniers will lose their hatred of Jews, global warming denialists will fight for the transition to a post-carbon economy, AIDS denialists and anti-vaxxers will campaign for access to life-saving drugs and vaccinations.

This may not be realistic. Assimilation is not the only alternative to denialism. There is another alternative; one that is dark and disturbing. It is already present, buried within the words and actions of denialists themselves. To understand it we must witness it directly. Only then can we decide not just whether there is a denier's alternative, but whether there should be.

6

– The Denier's Alternative –

Language can be made to do anything we want it to. It isn't beyond any denialist to say 'The Turks were right to exterminate the Armenians' or 'I am fine with the drowning of Bangladesh'. Words, though, are never just words. They are only speakable under certain conditions. As we have seen, the boundaries of permissible speech were broader in the past. Can we imagine a future in which the words that denialists avoid speaking could be speakable once again?

In this chapter, I want to demonstrate part of what is at stake in this question. I want to show what denialism seeks to prevent: the exposure of dark desire. It is only when we look directly at this darkness that we can grasp why it is so unspeakable and why denialists strain so hard to prevent its exposure.

This what I call the denier's alternative and it applies both to denialists and simple deniers.

Initially, I planned to set out the denier's alternative myself. I was going to write a defence of the Nazis and the Holocaust and its continued relevance as a model for future action against the Jews. I was going to write a plea for inaction against anthropogenic climate change that openly accepted both that it was happening and the immense suffering that inaction would cause.

Fictional ventriloquism has its limits. In the end, I couldn't write my own denier's alternative. How would I have felt if my words were circulated online by those who actually believed them? And, as a Jew, could I really write that I should be killed? This was just too morally compromising.

But I also came to realise that there was no *need* for fictional ventriloquism. As I immersed myself in denialist literature in preparing this book, it became clear to me that the denier's alternative was staring me in the face, hidden in plain sight. As I've already suggested, denialism is a failure to follow through the logic of one's arguments to the bitter end. A close look at denialist texts made me appreciate just how close to consummation denialism comes – the swerve often happens just a micrometre away from the end. Sometimes that is due to carelessness and lax use of language, exacerbated in the Internet age in the frenzy to get content online as quickly as possible. Sometimes it is the result of a more conscious kind of high-wire act: to come as close as possible to acknowledgement of the truth is to impress one's supporters and madden one's detractors.

In what follows, I will attempt to show that, by extracting such moments of near-acknowledgement from the words of denialists, it is possible to (re-) construct a denier's alternative. By liberating these fragments of naked desire from denialist obfuscation, I demonstrate that the denier's alternative is tantalisingly within sight. I have woven these fragments together into a coherent argument. When taken individually, in the context of a single denialist's *oeuvre*, they could easily be missed. When compiled collectively, they build into something unmistakable.

The quotations below are taken from the work of convinced denialists, from websites and publications that espouse denialism, and from individuals who have flirted with denialism. In constructing the denier's alternative from individual quotations, I appear to be engaging in the denialist art of 'quote-mining'. I can't deny the delicious irony of this. Yet whereas denialist quote-mining involves taking words out of context in order to support a conclusion that those who wrote or spoke them would never support, my own quote-mining aims to do the opposite: in denialism, it is only in isolated moments that the full force of their desire can be articulated. However, in order to make clear that these extracts are carefully extracted and that they are being used to construct an argument that their authors would not *openly* endorse, I have separated out individual quotes and included some italicised linking annotations and comments. In order to ensure consistency and readability, minor formatting changes have been made to some quotes.

I present two alternatives: one to climate change denialism and one to Holocaust denial. Alternatives to other denialisms could be constructed using a similar method.

THE GLOBAL WARMING DENIER'S ALTERNATIVE

We start with a view of creation. One reading of the biblical text appears to enjoin humans to extract as much value from the earth as they can. Creation is about us. 'Nature' and the rest of the non-human world exist only for our benefit.

God placed minerals, plants, and animals in and on the Earth for His pleasure, to reveal His glory and elicit man's praise, and to serve human needs through godly use.[1]

The ethic of conservation is the explicit abnegation of man's dominion over the Earth. The lower species are here for our use. God said so: Go forth, be fruitful, multiply, and rape the planet – it's yours. That's our job: drilling, mining and stripping. Sweaters are the anti-Biblical view. Big gas-guzzling cars with phones and CD players and wet bars – that's the Biblical view.[2]

Humans are innovators and creators. When we restrict our ability to exploit natural resources, we restrict something essential in ourselves.

— *The Denier's Alternative* —

Consider one central dimension of what it means to be human: the application of intelligence to overcome the obstacles that define life outside the Garden of Eden. The history of energy is a fundamental component of mankind's evolution, reflecting the inventiveness that is uniquely human.[3]

The humanist, which is the term I will use to describe someone on a human standard of value, treats the rest of nature as something to use for his benefit.[4]

The demand to 'restrict' technology is the demand to restrict man's mind. It is nature – i.e., reality – that makes both these goals impossible to achieve. Technology can be destroyed, and the mind can be paralysed, but neither can be restricted. Whenever and wherever such restrictions are attempted, it is the mind – not the state – that withers away.[5]

Humans should not constrain their ambition and creativity for the sake of the natural world. On the contrary, we owe the enormous gains we have made to our success in bolstering our control over nature. If anything, we need to take this process even further, rather than scaling back.[6]

If humans are our only concern in the world, it follows that nature must always be mute – it cannot be 'spoken for', defended or protected. It also follows that nature must be tied in to the human if it is to be considered at all. The only way to do this is to 'own' it. But ownership cannot be collective; nature does not belong to all humans, it can only belong to individual humans. To think otherwise is to restrict the potency of the individual, creative human mind.

In reality, there is no such thing as 'environmental issues.' There is only human conflict over the use of scarce resources. For example, if I start dumping toxic chemicals into your lake, and you object to it, this isn't really an environmental issue. Rather it is a dispute over the ownership of the lake. If I own the lake I can do with it as I please.[7]

And here we come to anthropogenic climate change. As with other environmental issues, it is our choice what we do to the non-human world. We do not have to think of it as a 'problem'.

If climate change is considered a problem, it does not follow automatically that it has to be stopped or minimised at whatever cost it takes. There is no natural duty to preserve the environment, which has no intrinsic value because valuations are products of mental activity. The most important entities for a human being are other human beings and not the environment.[8]

Not only does a concern for the environment undermine a human-centric view of the world, it also threatens to suffocate the precious creativity enshrined in capitalism. Climate change, and other environmental issues, could only be seriously addressed by extending the power of government over the individual and the free commerce between individuals. And that is reason enough not to address it.

Businesses should not be distracted and hijacked by social and political activists seeking to change perceived shortcomings of society's.[9]

Saving energy is not an appropriate goal for government regulation or even an important one.[10]

Of course, human life in the early twenty-first century is dependent on finite energy resources. In the future, we will have to transition to other forms of energy. Yet to make this transition would limit our human potency today. Just as we have no responsibilities towards the non-human environment, we have no responsibilities to as-yet-unborn humans.

Asking today's relatively poorer generations to reduce greenhouse gas emissions immediately for the benefit of future generations will essentially transfer wealth from today's poorer generations to tomorrow's wealthier and technologically better-endowed populations.

There may be a fossil-fuel-free world in the future, but now is not the future.[11]

We use fossil fuels . . . simply because they provide far and away the cheapest source of large-scale energy, and will continue to do so, no doubt not forever, but for the foreseeable future.[12]

The climate change that is being caused by our human activities will change the world. Some humans will have a greater ability to adapt to these changes than others. Those who are more exposed to climate risk and who have less resources to adapt, are not the responsibility of anyone but themselves.

If the sea level rises six inches, that's a big deal in the world, the Maldives might disappear or something, but OK, we can't mitigate that, we can't stop it.[13]

Because a clean, safe, healthful, beautiful environment is a costly good, wealthy societies can better afford environmental protection and restoration than poor societies.[14]

Low-latitude, developing countries must not wait for the free money to flow from rich countries in order to prepare for climate change. They must realise that they should adapt on their own to the looming changes and should strive, based on that realisation, to figure out and plan accordingly for the best ways their people and communities can adapt.[15]

There is nothing inevitable or 'natural' about worrying about the victims of climate change. To not care is, in fact, to uphold one's humanity. To care is to limit one's human potency.

The fact is that as much as people say they care, they don't act like they care one bit. I imagine there's a certain amount of emotional gratification in telling a pollster you're worried about global warming. What kind of deranged science-denying troglodyte isn't? But how you act tells us something, too. Most Americans don't feel obligated to make lifestyle changes. Maybe they don't really care at all, regardless of what they tell pollsters. Either way, it's great news for anyone concerned about genuine progress.[16]

People want wealth and comfort, not only for themselves but for others, too. They are unmoved by the campaign against climate change not because of its 'weirdo words' or complicated ideas, but because it is at root an elitist mission to convince us that our material desires are destroying the planet. Far from being irrational, the mass public apathy towards climate change that so freaks out eco-experts is entirely sensible and logical; in fact, it renews my faith in humankind.[17]

Not caring is, above all, an affirmation of individual liberty. By not acting to stall or prevent anthropogenic climate change we respect and honour freedom.

Liberty – true liberty – requires that people see themselves as self-respecting, self-determining subjects, capable of making free choices and pursuing the 'good life' as they see fit.[18]

Can it be right that people who have worked hard for their money should have it taken from them and then wasted in so spectacular fashion?[19]

Maybe the future will be uncomfortable, for all of us or just some of us. For now though . . .

The simple fact is that, if the world is warming, there is nothing we can do short of economic Armageddon to stop it. Let the seas rise. Let the wind blow. We can adapt. We are all going to die. Just not today. And in the meantime, I simply do not care about this issue.[20]

THE HOLOCAUST DENIER'S ALTERNATIVE

No one disputes that Jews have been persecuted for centuries. But why? The responsibility lies with the Jews.

Hundreds of years ago the Jews corrupted the [financial] system by getting control of gold, then gold mines, and forcing governments indebted to them to place their respective currencies on a gold standard, which funnily enough the Jews had in abundance, whilst pretending it was scarce. This created a shortage of money, forcing the populations to borrow it from the Jews at interest in order to make ends meet. There was always a natural conclusion to this cycle, the Jews obtaining all the wealth from the natives of the countries that they had enslaved to their usurious systems, the people realising they'd been ripped off and confronting the Jews about it (a legitimate confrontation that the Jews prefer to refer to as 'persecution'), and the Jews gathering up their ill-gotten gains, fleeing the country and settling in another to repeat the process.[21]

The Holocaust is therefore part of a cyclical, preordained pattern.

As we can see in the scriptures . . . the destiny of the Jews is to go from Genesis to genocide, receiving the Holocaust they truly fear and the one that is divinely ordained.[22]

Yet Jews are oblivious to their part in this process.

Somehow it doesn't dawn on them that maybe it is their unscrupulous behaviour that is the cause of hostility towards them in the first place.[23]

You never ask yourselves why you are disliked . . . It would never occur to you to look in the mirror and say 'why am I disliked, what is it the rest of humanity doesn't like about the Jewish people, to such an extent that they repeatedly put us through the grinder' . . . If you had behaved differently over the intervening 3,000 years the Germans would have gone about their business and not have found it necessary to go around doing whatever they did to you.[24]

The Holocaust needs to be reframed, as a response to a pernicious problem.

Why had the Nazis herded them into cattle cars and taken them to 'extermination camps' to dispose once and for all of the 'Jewish problem?'... If Hitler had developed a 'Final Solution' to the Jewish question, that there had to have been a 'Jewish Problem.'[25]

The communist Jews were intent on taking down an industrialised country (Germany) as another step toward global dominance, and almost succeeded.[26]

Something had to be done with these destructive anti-social Jews who were strangling Germany. Thanks to the Jews, Germany had lost its moral code and had become debased and de-cultured. Hitler observed the degrading machinations of the Jews in Austria and Germany. It not only disgusted and angered him, but saddened him to see how these two nations were being destroyed from the inside out like a cancer – a cancer that his sleepy folksmen could not see. The exact same angst those of us who are Jew-conscious find ourselves in. Throughout Hitler's political career, his common theme was about 'cleaning up'. He had seen the filth the Jews had created and desperately wanted Germany to reverse these degrading trends. Hitler recognised the Judaic invention of usury as unlawful, ungodly and unnatural – and as a Talmudic curse which has crippled every host nation the Jews have entered into and ultimately, that which brings about their demise. Hitler freed his people of this curse.[27]

The threat that Jews were responsible for in Germany is mirrored by the threat they pose today. Just as the Nazi response to them was justified at the time, so a similar response is justified today.

The Jews got everything they deserved. Persecution does not even rate in this endeavour. The 'German' Jews, if I were in charge, would have been executed, every single one of them, man, women & child, if they were proved to be traitors to Germany. The rest I would have put in prison camps. Why? Because I am no fool. I know what they were up to, sabotage and filthy dirty behaviour, just as they are promulgating in the United States of America and globally today. I make no apologies for it.[28]

The Nazi Holocaust is something to learn from, to be inspired by.

We're not going to get one over on the Jews – or anybody else – by denouncing our ancestors who also fought the Jews. The Jews are our enemy. Basically, the same forces Hitler and his people were up against then, are what we are up against now. This is becoming more and more clear to more and more people every day, as they look at the kiked out world around us and realise 'holy shit, *Hitler was right!*' And when Hitler fought these forces – the Jews, the capitalists, the communists, the international (((??media))) and (((banking systems))), and so on – he didn't try to take the easy route – and he wouldn't have gotten anywhere if he did. He fought our enemies head on, and he almost won. He showed us that they are not invincible – that they can be beaten . . . He bought us some time, and he showed us the way.[29]

There is no alternative. Hitler nearly destroyed the Jews; we must complete his work.

We have to realise that it is a WAR, war where there cannot be any compromises, we have to get rid of parasites who suck our blood, who rule us, and who kill us by millions. No co-existence, no cooperativeness. Our land should be free from aliens, children of our rulers should not rule our children![30]

These abominations, this outrage of lies and hatred, this hubris that one day or another destiny always comes to punish, in short, all these excesses must end.[31]

No matter how long it takes us and no matter to what lengths we must go, we'll demand a final settlement of the account between our two races . . . We'll go to the uttermost ends of the earth to hunt down the last of Satan's spawn.[32]

7

– The Post-Denialist Age –

Do we really want a world without denialism? It would be much more likely to produce the sort of language I presented in the last chapter than a universal language of moral consensus. Why should we expect 'defeated' denialists to crumple morally? After all, denialism is rarely an end in itself: it is a means of fighting for a vision of how the world should be when the dominant moral consensus seems to make that vision illegitimate. Desires, visions and dreams are much more difficult to let go of than the often tiresome work of explaining that glaciers are not really receding and Jews weren't really gassed.

Can we handle a world of radical moral diversity? Can we live with other human beings when the profound differences that divide us are out in the open? What would it be like to live next door to someone who can openly proclaim his wish for millions of people to die?

These are not hypothetical questions. It is starting to happen. We may be witnessing the birth pangs of the post-denialism world.

There has always been an excessiveness to denialism that can limit the success of the projects that it serves. To revise the very nature of scholarship and science to enable a particular end in one small and temporary corner of human existence seems like overkill. This excess can not only render denialists pariahs, it can put off timider potential supporters who have no desire for revolution. Thoughtful and politically astute denialists have recognised this limitation and pioneered what seem to be more nuanced, 'soft denialisms'.

One relatively longstanding soft denialism is 'intelligent design'.[1] Intelligent design theorists offer an alternative to evolution that seems more sophisticated and scholarly than a six-day creation period. Supposedly, the 'irreducible complexity' of many living things – the human eye is often mentioned – is such that it is implausible to suggest that their manifold constituent parts could have emerged over time. The extraordinary 'fine tuning' of life and the universe in which it exists could only have emerged as a conscious act by a 'designer' – the word 'God' is not always mentioned – with an overall plan. While intelligent design theory became a fully-fledged denialist school relatively recently, it draws on deep theological roots going back centuries. Its great advantage is that it can impress and wrong-foot through unabashed scientific language, without the obvious absurdities of 'young earth' creationism. There is a coy reticence to intelligent design, that seems to prove that the universe was designed without offering a complete theory of, or evidence for, who or what that designer is. Ultimately then, for all its surface reasonableness, it has not succeeded in overturning evolution, although it might have offered a more comfortable home for those theists who cannot accept evolution but baulk at attempts to prove the world was created in six days.

Another soft denialism involves 'relativising' the Holocaust. Holocaust deniers have long attempted to combine the minimisation of Jewish deaths at the hands of the Nazis with highlighting allied war atrocities, such as the bombing of Dresden in 1945 and the savage treatment of German civilians by the advancing Russians. Such a strategy can still pay dividends even without denying the Holocaust of the Jews. Both left- and right-wingers may point to non-Jewish victims of the Nazi mass murder, such as Roma, homosexuals and civilians from many countries, as a way of challenging the uniqueness of the Holocaust. Of course, it is perfectly legitimate to compare the Jewish Holocaust to other genocides and atrocities, but when it is part of a project that aims to use non-Jewish dead as a way of undermining Jewish memorialisation, it becomes much more sinister. In some eastern European countries, such as Poland and Lithuania, the memorialisation of the murder of non-Jewish victims by the Soviets can become a way of marginalising Jewish victims as well as erasing troubling questions regarding local participation in the Holocaust. Without actually denying the murder of Jews, soft denialism can be as, if not more, effective than full-blown denialism in rehabilitating non-German genocidaires at least.[2] It only requires a relatively small twist on what are incontrovertible historical facts to do so.

Those opposed to action on global warming have also used soft denialism effectively. Not only is opposition to action on anthropogenic global warming a diverse coalition, the multi-dimensional complexity of the science and the knottiness of policy solutions are such that there are a multitude of possible approaches to denialism. Whereas for some denialists the very notion of anthropogenic climate change is anathema, for others a more pragmatic approach is more palatable. After all, it is still possible to preserve the current mode of carbon-based capitalism as long as possible with the awareness that, at some point, the party will be over.

Within the field of global warming denialism, quasi-acknowledgements are slowly becoming more common, gradually conceding the science over time, while still not giving up political and moral priorities. There is a kind of order to the claims made over time by global warming denialists:

1 Anthropogenic global warming isn't possible.
2 Anthropogenic global warming is possible but is not happening.
3 Global warming is happening, but it isn't anthropogenic.
4 Anthropogenic global warming is happening, but it isn't a problem.

5 Anthropogenic global warming is happening, but it is a problem we can adapt to and there are more serious problems that humanity should address as a priority.
6 Anthropogenic global warming is happening and causing serious problems but it is too late to do anything about it other than adapt.

1) is now becoming rarer, and the dominant trend in denialism is to assert 2) while moving gradually towards 3) and 4). At the other end of the scale, 6) is rare but will likely become more prevalent over the next few decades. 4) and 5) are the 'avant garde' of global warming denialism and are being proposed by advocates who seem to lack the intimidating intensity of other denialists. They profess some level of care for the environment and certainly emphasise their concern for humanity in the developing world. They do not pose as Galileos fighting a scientific establishment, but as urbane and subtle individuals who merely differ on the interpretation of scientific evidence.

Bjorn Lomborg is one of the most influential of these soft deniers.[3] The 'Copenhagen Consensus' that he has developed sees anthropogenic global warming as but one issue that impacts on the global south, one for which cost-benefit analysis suggests should not be the priority. Lomborg has been criticised for using denialist techniques to minimise the costs of global warming, albeit techniques of a subtler (and perhaps, therefore, more pernicious) variety than more implacable denialists do.[4] Yet Lomborg remains an attractive figure, coming across as open-minded, non-conspiratorial and speaking fluently the language of liberal concern for those on the sharp end of globalised capitalism. There is a similarly positive air around those who have been called the 'new optimists', such as Matt Ridley, who brim with enthusiasm for the ability of capitalism to raise living standards and adapt to changes such as global warming.[5] Alex Epstein, in his book *The Moral Case for Fossil Fuels*, argues that the carbon-based economy remains the best chance for humans as a species to thrive and flourish long into the future.[6]

Such soft denialisms are based on misconceptions – particularly that capitalism can result in indefinite material improvement – that are no less dangerous than their harder cousins. Perhaps they will prove more politically efficacious in providing alibis for global warming inaction. But one can't help wondering if they will also prove frustrating and disappointing for those committed to harder forms of denialism. Indeed, the global warming denialist community has always been a coalition between a number of competing voices, some of whom are more pragmatically minded than others. As pragmatists, soft denialists are simply making what they feel is the argument that can get the most traction with the most people. Similarly, the oil industry largely draws on the most effective strategies that will protect its commercial viability – hard denialist, soft denialist or not denialist at all. There are signs that the global warming denialist community is under increasing tension as the oil industry and other pragmatists recoil from their more ideologically committed bedfellows.[7] In 2017, James Delingpole, a prominent global warming denialist, castigated those in the oil industry who would make any compromise to the environmentalists:

> Almost everyone at a senior level in Big Oil is a craven, simpering, politically correct, spineless, surrender-monkey corporate shill. They're cowards who are scared of free markets, won't speak up for capitalism, won't even defend their core business.
> [. . .]
> If Big Oil won't speak out for the oil industry, who will?
> Sadly, the burden invariably falls to that small group of maverick believers in free markets and honest science who don't care about all the brickbats they get for being defenders of 'dirty fuel' because they'd rather speak the truth than be popular.[8]

In any case, even the thrills of hard denialism may not be enough for some. However excessive denialism might be, it still requires discipline. Denialism has traditionally mimicked the sober institutions of legitimate scholarship. In the past, even to gain access to denialist thought you had to be part of the right circles or actively seek them out. These days, dissemination is almost cost-free and anyone who uses social media will find denialism hard to avoid. More than that: these days, everyone can become a publisher, developing individual twists on denialist thought.

The emergence of a 'post-truth' world in which everyone chooses what facts to believe has been widely reported.[9] What is less commented on is that denialist scholarship can also be undermined in the post-truth era. A symptom of this is the proliferation of 'multi-denialists' who reject not just one but a whole range of sciences and scholarly consensuses. The standard denialist strategy has been to focus on one particular area, in part to demonstrate that denialists are not against all kinds of scholarship. The restraint this requires is weakening in the connected age. One example of this is the '9/11 truth movement', which has never managed to institutionalise and develop an orthodoxy in the way that pre-Internet denialisms did.[10] Those who believe that the 'official story' of the 9/11 attacks was a lie can believe that elements in the US government had foreknowledge of the attacks but let them happen, or that the attacks were deliberately planned and carried out by the government, or that Jews/Israel/Mossad were behind it, or that shadowy forces in the 'New World Order' were behind it – or some cocktail of all of these. They can believe that the towers were brought down by controlled demolition, or that no planes hit the towers, or that there were no floors in the towers, or that there were no passengers in the planes – or some combination of all of these.

Truthers can believe in all kinds of other conspiracy theories and denialisms. The notorious US radio host Alex Jones, as well as questioning the 9/11 attacks, advocates everything from global warming denialism to conspiracy theories about fake moon landings.

This undisciplined creativity offers manifold opportunities for denialism to develop in new directions. It also allows older, seemingly moribund, denialisms to be revived. Flat earth theories are one example. From the classical period onwards, the belief in a flat earth was generally rejected by educated people and it was in the post-Enlightenment period that it was reborn, an early form of revolt against experts and the increasingly baffling findings of modern science.[11] By the 1960s it was largely a joke, supported by a tiny minority of cranks. Yet today flat earth theories are proliferating again. While some of them have developed the kind of exceptionally convoluted 'proofs' familiar from other denialisms, the quasi-scholarly veneer is usually much thinner than in the denialist mainstream. Rather, flat earthers express their joyful hopes in a much more direct way:

Because it's not true, in the boring, conventional sense of the word, Flat Earth theory has an enormous creative potential: all those thousands of people, constantly creating their crystalline new realities and uploading them to YouTube. Flat Earth is fascinating because in an era where so much of the world is disenchanting and so much of social existence is already a given – you will have your job, you will have your life, you will be exploited and then you will die – there are people who can dream the Earth itself into a different shape. It's flat.[12]

While we appear to be witnessing both an intensification and broadening of denialism, online proliferation is also pushing it so far that it is beginning to fall apart. Denialism isn't creating new, alternative orthodoxies so much as obliterating the very idea of orthodoxy. The collective, institutional work of building a substantial bulwark against scholarly consensus gives way to a kind of free-for-all that may be exciting to those involved in it, but is also more superficial and easier to debunk.

While denialism has never been more vital or self-confident, this vital self-confidence is demonstrated through a weakening of its structures. Take Donald Trump's famous tweet of 6 November 2012: 'The concept of global warming was created by and for the Chinese in order to make U.S. manufacturing non-competitive.' While Trump has cast doubt on global warming subsequent to that tweet, he has not pushed the claim that the concept was created by the Chinese. This is not a claim regularly made by 'mainstream' global warming denialists, although it may be a garbled version of the argument that global climate treaties will unfairly weaken the US economy at the expense of the Chinese. Like much of Donald Trump's discourse, the tweet was simply thrown into the world, without the sustained toil that denialists usually engage in to build an organised counter-consensus. Yet this lazy denialism is not simply a retreat to an earlier or more primitive kind of reflexive denial, shorn of the sophistry of denialism. Rather, it rests on the security than comes from knowing that generations of denialists have created enough doubt already; all that people like Trump need to do is to signal vaguely in a denialist direction.

I call this emerging phenomenon 'post-denialism'. It draws on a longstanding undercurrent of resistance to the conditions that brought about denialism in the first place. Not everyone acquiesced to the stultifying moral consensus in modernity. Not everyone wanted to bridge the gap. In an illuminating article, David Garland has argued that the epidemic of lynching in the US southern states in the early twentieth century was brought about by a refusal to abandon one's expressive hatred in favour of the sober language of justice:

The public torture lynching was invented, at the turn of the twentieth century, to communicate impassioned sentiments that could no longer be expressed in the official idiom of the criminal law, and to inflict a level of suffering that had long since been officially disavowed.[13]

The philosopher Ayn Rand was also someone who found modern pieties unappealing. In her 'objectivist' philosophy, she proclaimed 'selfishness' as the highest ideal. For Rand, there was little need for the veneer of pretence that capitalist individualism could lead to wider social goods. Rather, the fulfilment of man's (*sic*) potency overrode everything else. Rand was perfectly comfortable with openly expressing her indifference to the suffering caused by such things as the genocide of Native Americans and environmental pollution.[14] Those on the US political right, who have been influenced by Rand, such as Alan Greenspan and Rand Paul, are more polished, less prepared to openly proclaim their own selfish egoism. Rand's own confrontational life, in which she alienated many of her closest followers, represents a model few would wish to follow.[15] Nonetheless, she offers a precedent for a post-denialist way of being that is unafraid to speak of one's darker desires without shame.

One of the most striking features about Donald Trump has been his lack of shame. While a certain degree of shamelessness is probably inevitable and necessary for political leaders – unlike Bill Clinton, most of us would have crawled into a hole when publicly confronted with the sordid details of our philandering – Trump's degree of shamelessness may be unprecedented for a head of state in a democratic nation. Whatever the eventual consequences of his well-documented profiteering, the misogyny, abusiveness, ignorance and so on, his ability to show up in public day after day knowing what is known about him sets an extraordinary precedent. If you have the guts to stand tall when your 'locker room' brutality is exposed, when your fundamental incompetence is repeatedly revealed, why would you pretend to care about such trifles as climate catastrophe?

At some point a leader of a Western democracy was inevitably going to refuse to be ashamed any more. The ground was prepared for Trump by the denialist-ridden American right; all he had to do was to push a little harder. Take torture: the George W. Bush administration took a giant step towards the legitimation of torture in a democratic society through the open approval of waterboarding of Islamist militants. True, it was still cloaked in the euphemism of 'enhanced interrogation' and Dick Cheney among others still denies this constituted torture.[16] Yet we now have the situation in which James E. Mitchell, who personally conducted some of the waterboarding, can publish a book openly defending his actions.[17] And on the campaign trail in November 2015, Donald Trump went even further than the Bush administration:

Would I approve waterboarding? You bet your ass I would. In a heartbeat. I would approve more than that. It works . . . and if it doesn't work, they deserve it anyway for what they do to us.[18]

More generally, the following well-known passage from a 2004 article by Ron Suskind (reporting a quote widely attributed to Karl Rove), sums up an approach to the world that undergirds both denialism and post-denialism:

> The aide said that guys like me were 'in what we call the reality-based community,' which he defined as people who 'believe that solutions emerge from your judicious study of discernible reality.' I nodded and murmured something about Enlightenment principles and empiricism. He cut me off. 'That's not the way the world really works anymore,' he continued. 'We're an empire now, and when we act, we create our own reality. And while you're studying that reality – judiciously, as you will – we'll act again, creating other new realities, which you can study too, and that's how things will sort out. We're history's actors . . . and you, all of you, will be left to just study what we do.'[19]

The new order Rove yearned for is one in which there is no gap between desire and action, between desire and what is legitimately desirable. Denialism provides a stepping stone towards this world, post-denialism goes one step further.

Post-denialism isn't just desire unleashed, it is desire armed. Denialism may work well as an oppositional strategy, but it is much less necessary once in power. When denialists come into government they have more freedom to fall back on lazy forms of denial that simply wave away inconvenient truths. Governments can purge their websites of references to climate change, issue gag rules to scientists and close down research centres.[20] Again, this self-confident silencing did not materialise overnight. Denialist politicians and lobbyists laboured for decades within the US administration to erode the threatening prestige of scientific research. Chris Mooney has detailed the ways that US Republicans worked for years to marginalise scientific expertise.[21] For example, the 1996 abolition of the US Congress's Office of Technology Assessment (during the Clinton presidency but in the period of Newt Gingrich's 'contract with America'), constituted a deliberate turning away from scientific expertise under the guise of eliminating government wastefulness.

Of course, such actions were carried out by denialists in the name of science. Post-denialism is closer to straightforward denial in its lack of concern for scholarly validation. Further, in post-denialism, there is greater freedom to redefine not just science but knowledge itself. While denialism may simply wish to replace one set of experts with another, in practice the constant undermining of mainstream expertise can pave the way for a new and radical approach to knowledge. In this approach, scholarship and empirical research are treated as an impediment to knowledge. To know something is to feel the force of an unmediated truth that is available to all those who are open-minded enough to receive it – and it is the ordinary masses with their unpolluted minds that are most able to do this. As Melanie Phillips argues:

While the ordinary people appear to be connected to reality and able to tell fact from fantasy and right from wrong, it is the intelligentsia – supposedly the custodians of reason – who seem to be taking the most irrational, prejudiced and intolerant positions, clothed nevertheless in the most high-minded concerns of 'progressive' politics.[22]

The post-denialist concept of truth is one in which the individual is the arbiter of what is truthful. This is a deeper kind of truth that persists beyond what an individual says and what happens in the world around. As Faisal Devji argues, sincerity is the all-important criterion for judging truth claims in this brave new world:

Sincerity has no need for . . . external authorities. Sincerity requires no external validation. It must be judged in an entirely self-referential way. Curiously, this means that it doesn't need to adhere to any deeply held belief either. It can be shallow, it can even be withdrawn from any previous claim. For, based as it is on fundamental doubt, sincerity is most important when it is concerned with relatively minor and lightly held beliefs, such as that regarding Obama's birthplace.[23]

Truth becomes a kind of primal force, almost beyond words, certainly beyond facts. It becomes a feeling (what Stephen Colbert memorably described as 'truthiness'), a sense that only those with unpolluted minds possess. As in wrestling, where audience and grapplers collude in producing a spectacle simultaneously real and unreal (a practice known as 'kayfabe'), the constant collaborative effort to create this new truth helps to make it real – almost.[24]

Not a few commentators have argued that this playful attitude to reality seems to echo, and may even have been brought about by, postmodern deconstructions of the notion of truth.[25] Certainly it would seem that sections of the political right are effectively weaponising the malleable nature of language. Yet one can equally say that this new epistemology is the result of tendencies within the Enlightenment project itself. The Enlightenment lauded the potential of individual reason to penetrate the mysteries of existence and conquer nature. This might have seemed possible in the eighteenth century, in which gifted polymaths could deal with a relatively manageable canon of knowledge. In our age of hyper-complex intellectual specialisation, such hopes are foolish:

> we live in an age in which the vast bulk of knowledge can only be accessed in mediated forms which rely on the testimony of various specialists. Contemporary approaches to epistemology, however, remain anchored in the intellectual ideals of the Enlightenment. These demand first-hand inquiry, independent thinking, and a scepticism about information passed down by authorities and experts. As such, we may find ourselves attempting to use an epistemological schema radically unsuited to a world whose staggering material complexity involves an unprecedented degree of specialisation and knowledge mediation.[26]

Both denialism and post-denialism are more firmly rooted in the Enlightenment tradition than many would like to admit. They both involve a fervent commitment to an idea of truth. Where post-denialism parts ways from denialism is in its almost mystical belief in truth beyond language, beyond external reality.

And yet . . . post-denialism is also more capable of producing an honest admission of desire than denialism. There is an odd duality here: in post-denialism, there is scope for raw, brutal acknowledgement and also wilder fantasies with little hold on reality. It is 'sincerity' that persists across this duality. Post-denialism can seem utterly unmoored from reality and violently unpredictable; but it has a strange integrity that means that, for those who practise it, it has a surprising coherence.

Post-denialism has not yet supplanted denialism. Denialism is beginning to be questioned by some of its practitioners (or those who, in a previous generation, might have been practitioners), as they take tentative steps towards a new age. This is particularly evident on the racist far right, where the dominance of Holocaust denial is beginning to erode. Nicholas Terry summarises seven reasons for this:

1. Consistent social disapproval
2. Political ineffectiveness
3. The ease of finding other ways of expressing anti-Semitism or delegitimising Israel

4. Loss of 'market share' to other conspiracy theories
5. Inability to cope with the volume of recent Holocaust research
6. Lack of novelty
7. The ageing of the movement[27]

Holocaust deniers remain pariahs in most countries. Memorialisation of the Holocaust in Western countries has become more significant, culturally and politically (for example, with the opening of the United States Holocaust Memorial Museum in 1993, and the institution of Holocaust Memorial Day in the UK in 2001). No wonder then that Marc Weber, onetime director of the Institute for Historical Review, glumly concluded in 2009 that Holocaust denial had become irrelevant.[28] Some Holocaust deniers have even recanted, expressing their frustration with the movement and acknowledging that many of its claims are simply untenable, as Eric Hunt, previously a producer of widely circulated online videos denying the Holocaust, did in 2016.[29]

Yet such admissions of defeat are not the end of the story. They are not accompanied by a retreat from antisemitism. Marc Weber treats the failures of Holocaust denial as a consequence of the nefarious power of the Jews:

In short, the Holocaust assumed an important role in the social-cultural life of America and western Europe in keeping with, and as an expression of, a phenomenal increase in Jewish influence and power. The Holocaust 'remembrance' campaign is not so much a source of Jewish-Zionist power as it is an expression of it. For that reason, debunking the Holocaust will not shatter that power.

Suppose *The New York Times* were to report tomorrow that Israel's Yad Vashem Holocaust center and the US Holocaust Memorial Museum had announced that no more than one million Jews died during World War II, and that no Jews were killed in gas chambers at Auschwitz. The impact on Jewish-Zionist power would surely be minimal.[30]

And for Eric Hunt, Holocaust denial was ultimately a distraction from the real task:

In many ways, I feel the 'denial' issue held me back from tackling other issues essential to the survival of Western Civilisation. Especially Nationalism, race realism, and opposing the very real Jewish-led white genocide campaign.[31]

Notably, many of the leading lights in the emerging constellation of far-right intellectuals that has gained prominence in recent years, such as Kevin MacDonald and Nick Land, are not Holocaust deniers or, if they are, they do not emphasise it in their work. Such developments are a tacit acknowledgement that, while Holocaust denial might have outlived its usefulness as a strategy, in our new age there are new possibilities for relating to the Holocaust. As I have argued, one of the reasons why Holocaust denial emerged was that genocide could not be publicly legitimated. While the open celebration of genocide might still be rare and marginal, today there are more opportunities for the expression of the kind of strategic apathy that has long been common in relating to other genocides that are somehow 'inconvenient'.

On 27 January 2017 President Trump issued a statement for International Holocaust Memorial Day that seemed to avoid making specific mention of the Jews killed:

It is with a heavy heart and somber mind that we remember and honour the victims, survivors, heroes of the Holocaust. It is impossible to fully fathom the depravity and horror inflicted on innocent people by Nazi terror.

The statement was widely criticised, including by many Jewish leaders and opinion formers, for generalising the Holocaust out of existence.[32] Richard Spencer, a prominent alt-right figure, strongly approved of the statement and criticised the Jewish response for the same reason:

This week, the activist Jewish community in the United States forcefully reminded the world that, no matter how much we might moralise the Holocaust, no matter how much we might glean from it lessons about man's fallen state or dehumanisation in the modern world, the Holocaust is all about the Jews. It is all about their meta-narrative of suffering, and it shall undergird their peculiar position in American society, and theirs alone.

If the Holocaust is seen as just one instance of genocide, then it will, as Spencer puts it, 'dethrone Jews from a special position in the universe'. While there is nothing antisemitic about understanding the Holocaust in the context of the study of genocide and one can make nuanced arguments that the growing memorialisation of the Holocaust raises some troubling questions, for the antisemitic far right, this is not enough.[33] Relativising the Holocaust can pave the way for encouraging apathy towards its victims, which may pave the way for seeing the Holocaust as somehow deserved, which may pave the way for conducting a future genocide. Certainly, plenty of online trolls enjoy taunting Jews over the gas chambers.[34]

Post-denialism allows for sly allusions, for nudges and winks, for ambiguity. It's no coincidence that antisemites who have Jewish origins are particularly adept at this. They might be drawn to Holocaust denial, but they can never quite take the final step. One example is the Israeli-born musician and writer Gilad Atzmon:

What is the Holocaust religion there to conceal? As long as we fail to ask questions, we will be subjected to Zionists and their Neocons agents' plots ... Holocaust religion robs humanity of its humanism. For the sake of peace and future generations, the Holocaust must be stripped of its exceptional status immediately. It must be subjected to thorough historical scrutiny. Truth and truth-seeking is an elementary human experience. It must prevail.[35]

The call for 'truth' is common in denialist discourse, but Atzmon uses a creative ambiguity here and elsewhere in his work to obfuscate whether he is talking about the Holocaust as a historical event or the Holocaust as a 'religion'. Israel Shamir, a Russian-Swedish journalist who claims to be of Jewish descent and to have served in the Israeli army, was similarly ambiguous in a 2011 interview with a Jewish publication:

So, Auschwitz as being a place to exterminate Jews ...
This idea came to existence only after the war.
So, it's a rumour?
No, no, no. I don't say that at all. No.
But you said, 'the rumor of mass annihilation.'
I can repeat more clear. I am not all that interested in what was in reality. I am interested in perceptions. Something I am dealing with is perceptions. So, perceptions during the war was that it was quite awful deportation camp, where people were deported and kept, worked hard labour, this sort of thing. That's how it was perceived. Only after the war, different perception came. And that was a perception of mass annihilation, and mass murder, and all that.
So, it's not a fact that there was mass annihilation?
[. . .]
That's, not, I did not say that at all. I didn't even say that, I didn't even intend to say this or other way. What I say is that there was no such perception during the war. This perception came after the war.
But so which one is true?
I am not even interested in this kind of question. That is something that is very much outside of my interest.

But can you comment about if these concentration camps were for mass murder?
Ah, I have really no knowledge about it at all. I was not interested in it because I reject the idea that it is important, you see?[36]

The noisy dogmatism of Holocaust denial is replaced here by a kind of aggressive uncertainty, a violent apathy, a loud silence. As a strategy, this can wrong-foot and confuse opponents. It enables all kinds of strange alliances that might not have been possible for a straight denialist. Atzmon, for example, has admirers on both the far left and the far right.

We also see this strategy wielded with particular brilliance in Putin's Russia, where an ambiguous kind of authoritarianism means that its citizens never know what is permitted at any particular point. As Peter Pomerantsev, one of its sharpest observers, argues:

Moscow can feel like an oligarchy in the morning and a democracy in the afternoon, a monarchy for dinner and a totalitarian state by bedtime.[37]

Indeed, Putin's Russia has played an important part in bringing about post-denialism in the West. Aside from the possible role Russia played in hacking the 2016 US election, it has fostered the growth of a politics that is simultaneously left wing and right wing, that gathers in both leftist anti-imperialists who yearn for Russia to undermine the West, as well as those on the right who lust after its sexual conservatism and its oligarchical possibilities.

This new politics is constantly shifting and bewildering. As Angela Nagle observed in *Kill All Normies*, this delight at throwing people off balance isn't just difficult to respond to, it is thrilling for those who take part in it:

> The throwing off of the id that characterised this transgressive countercultural tradition also characterised sites like 4chan, and its culture of trolling and taboo-breaking anti-moral humour, which is often described as insane or unhinged to baffled outsiders.[38]

This unleashing of desire doesn't take coherent form, it is beyond sense, as Peter Pomerantsev observed in the wake of Trump's victory in the US:

> This is a (dark) joy. All the madness you feel, you can now let it out and it's okay. The very point of Trump is to validate the pleasure of spouting shit, the joy of pure emotion, often anger, without any sense. And an audience which has already spent a decade living without facts can now indulge in a full, anarchic liberation from coherence.[39]

At the same time, we are not quite at a situation in which pure desire can be expressed. As Nagle argued in piece written in August 2017, after her book was published but in the wake of the riots in Charlottesville, the free-wheeling milieu she described has been beset with uncertainty: once real violence and genuine fascism becomes resurgent, those who delighted in the language of hate have to confront whether or not this is what they really want – and for some at least, it stops being fun.[40] In any case, there has always been a streak of vulnerability that accompanies trolling. As has often been pointed out, those who taunt the offended with accusation of being 'snowflakes' can be remarkably sensitive to anything resembling criticism.[41]

While the barriers that prevented the open expression of desire have been eroded, there remains a gap between desire and action that can be hard to cross. The prevalence of humour on the alt-right, albeit of the hateful variety, sometimes acts in a similar way to denialism: as an alibi, a barrier to facing up to the consequences of desire. The emerging post-denialism may hasten the day when the Holocaust is openly celebrated, when victims of climate change are left to their fate, when medicine and science are rejected without excuses, but post-denialism itself still retains elements of the denialism that paved the way for it.

To find the truly naked denier's alternative, we have to look outside Western democracies. As I have argued, denialism never took as firm a hold in non-Western developing countries, particularly those with an authoritarian tradition. It is outside the West that models for the abandonment of denialism can be found.

In September 2016 President Rodrigo Duterte of the Philippines was quoted as saying:

Hitler massacred three million Jews. Now there is three million, what is it, three million drug addicts [in the Philippines] there are. I'd be happy to slaughter them. At least if Germany had Hitler, the Philippines would have [me]. You know my victims. I would like them to be all criminals, to finish the problem of my country and save the next generation from perdition.[42]

Duterte has made no secret of the extra-judicial murders of drug dealers, drug users and other assorted enemies, that he has presided over – indeed, he has celebrated them. James Fenton contrasts the killing of opposition leader Ninoy Aquino in 1983 under President Marcos with the actions of Duterte today:

in the case of Ninoy, a certain lip service was paid to due process. An alibi was carefully prepared... When the postmortem contradicted the official story, an alternative postmortem was sought and found. There was some sense lingering in Marcos's circle of what a respectable outcome would look like, even if respectability was not achieved.

Today by contrast the pretense of due process is impossible, because the man at the top simply blows it away. One of Duterte's chief selling points as a leader is that he doesn't give a shit.[43]

Duterte may or may not have been a denialist had

— *The Post-Denialist Age* —

he been in power in the 1980s, but he is joyfully rejecting denialism today. And in May 2017, Donald Trump praised Duterte for 'doing a great job'.[44] Perhaps there was some envy here?

Another, even more extreme, model of unrestrained and proud brutality, is that of Islamic State. Whatever its long-term political legacy, it has provided a model not just for a government that kills, tortures, rapes and enslaves – after all, plenty of other states do that – but that actively promotes such actions. There is no denialism or post-denialism here: just delight at savagery, where the promise of killing, enslaving and rape is actively used to attract prospective fighters. While established states in the region might be appalled at the threat Islamic State has posed to them, might there not also be a sly envy in some quarters? Might there not be a yearning among Qatari moguls to indulge in undisguised slave ownership, rather than setting up impenetrable webs of indentured sub-contractors so as to preserve a fig-leaf of respectability for the benefit of FIFA and other over-sensitive international organisations?

In the West, it is still necessary to look to the fringes to find an embrace of dark desires without the hedging of denialism or post-denialism. While there is a long tradition of exploring transgression within the arts, this has generally been accompanied by an avoidance of anything that can be construed as an overt political agenda. In my research on extreme heavy metal scenes, even the openly fascistic margins of the spectrum tend to eschew the political, with some exceptions.[45] Satanic, occultist and esoteric writers, artists and practitioners have, at times, openly lauded mass killing, rape and the rejection of compassion, but for the most part they haven't done anything about it and their influence remains small.[46] While in recent years there has been a resurgence of intellectual interest in non-democratic thought – in the work of the 'dark enlightenment' thinker Nick Land for example – its cryptic and esoteric nature tends to prevent the overt celebration of suffering.[47]

Still, there are signs of an emerging willingness to drop all barriers to direct expression of hatred. The recent scrutiny of far-right movements has inevitably revealed statements that might once have remained unspoken, or only been spoken behind closed doors. In August 2017 for example, one KKK leader told a journalist: 'We killed 6 million Jews the last time. Eleven million is nothing'.[48] A piece published by the *Daily Stormer* before the August 2017 Charlottesville far-right rally ended:

Next stop: Charlottesville, VA.
Final stop: Auschwitz.[49]

Indeed, the *Daily Stormer*, one of the most prominent online publications of the resurgent far-right, demonstrates an exuberant agility in balancing denialism, post-denialism and open hatred simultaneously, using humour as a method of floating between them all. But there is no doubt what the ultimate destination is. As Andrew Anglin, who runs the site, put it, in a leaked style guide for contributors:

The unindoctrinated should not be able to tell if we are joking or not. There should also be a conscious awareness of mocking stereotypes of hateful racists. I usually think of this as self-deprecating humour – I am a racist making fun of stereotypes of racists, because I don't take myself super-seriously.

This is obviously a ploy and I actually do want to gas kikes. But that's neither here nor there.[50]

Denialists are transitioning to post-denialism and beyond at different rates (and some are not transitioning at all). Perhaps the racist far right are the avant-garde here. While other denialists may be appalled at post-denialist callousness about the Holocaust, they will all inevitably be influenced by the weakening of the restraint against the open expression of desires.

For all these reasons, we need to consider the denier's alternative as more than hypothetical. And that means considering how to respond to it.

8

– An Alternative –

This has not been a very helpful book, has it? I'm sure I haven't endeared myself to any denialists. I've liberally used the term denialist, lumping a whole swathe of people together under the same dismal umbrella. I've hardly even attempted to debunk their arguments. I've presumed to tell them what they really desire. I've taunted them to openly embrace horrifying beliefs that they insist they do not hold. I've even presumed to empathise with their 'predicament'.

Neither have I given much credit to those who have toiled to debunk denialist claims. I've offered precious little hope that denialism can give way to truthful acknowledgement. My view of humanity seems to be pretty low. And then I say that something even worse than denialism has appeared on the horizon.

My argument seems to have led me to a hopeless place: one where we either accept denialism as a permanent feature of the world, or open ourselves up to a world in which all manner of appalling desires can be freely spoken of. Have I been too harsh?

There's certainly a strain of hopelessness running through anti-denialist discourse. In particular, campaigners against anthropogenic global warming

— An Alternative —

can and do feel despair that, as the task becomes ever more urgent, so denialism continues to run rampant (along with apathy and softer forms of denial). It appears that nothing works in the campaign to make humanity aware of the threat it faces.[1] Certainly, the voice of liberal, technocratic reason, with all its graphs, diagrams and impeccable rationality, is increasingly ignored:

In the face of these epochal changes, the superego of managerial liberalism is impotent. On some level it knows that. But it cannot simply abdicate, and it will take a while yet for it to wither entirely away. In the meantime, all it can do is blather, make empty threats of guilt and shame, issue fact-checks and explainers, shout from the roadside to an indifferent planet as the whole world goes libidinal and mad.[2]

Or to put it another way:

We're fucked. The only questions are how soon and how badly.[3]

In some environmentalist circles, there is a growing awareness that emphasising statistics, policy and technology is not an effective way of convincing people of the seriousness of the situation and the need for radical change. Writers such as Paul Kingsnorth have instead argued that we need new narratives, embedded in compelling stories, that can reframe the world.[4] More generally, research in psychology and neuroscience has shown how emotions, feelings and stories may be more important in making political judgements than sober evaluations of policy. As Drew Westen argues, one of the reasons why technocrats such as Al Gore have been electorally unsuccessful in recent years is that they are poor at mobilising direct appeals to the emotions.[5] Jonathan Haidt has similarly argued that in order to be convincing, appeals to other 'moral tribes' need to be made in ways that are empathetic and in tune with their moral worlds.

The implication of such research is that debunking is not just largely ineffective, it's also too late. By the time denialism has been built up, it creates an impregnable barrier that cannot be breached by rational argument. However, a recent research paper suggests that the 'backfire effect' – when correcting erroneous facts actually leads to an increased belief in them – may be less widespread than some researchers have suggested.[6] Further, as a 2017 study showed, in some cases it is possible to 'inoculate' people against denialist arguments, if you can reach them before their views are fully formed, by explaining *how* denialists argue.[7] Further, early education on the scientific method and education for experts on how to effectively communicate research might pay dividends.[8] Educators need to frame their arguments in a way that is appropriate to their audience.

Civility might also help. While it's probably true

— *An Alternative* —

that hardcore denialist activists may be resistant to any kind of argument, there may well be waverers who are open to other arguments. A hostile approach could close down the possibility of gaining 'converts'. One science writer offered twenty-two short and civil answers to twenty-two creationist arguments, including:

9) If God did not create everything, how did the first single-celled organism originate? By chance?
This is a question where I'm proud to say 'I don't know.' Because it's true: I don't, but perhaps someday we will! You are asking one of the biggest questions of all: how did life come to exist in this world? And the answer is that – right now – we don't know. But scientists are working on it. There's a lot that we do know that's related to that question, but the big one – how we went from non-life to life in the Universe – is still an open one. I hope I live long enough to be there when we figure this puzzle out; don't you? [9]

Whether or not such responses work in the sense of making converts, they are at least open to the possibility being heard amongst all the online sound and fury. Modest self-effacement might be a much better strategy than constantly banging on about the 'truth'. As Emma Jane and Chris Fleming have argued, it is precisely the Enlightenment insistence on the possibility of truth being out there, waiting to be discovered by the determined scholar, that emboldens both conspiracist and debunker. Acknowledging uncertainty and ignorance may cut the ground out from under the denialist's feet:

> Perhaps now is a good time – and perhaps it may always be a good time – to inscribe naiveté as an epistemological ideal, to admit that we know less than what we think we do [. . .] Perhaps we should occasionally stop and say to ourselves, 'You know, maybe I have absolutely no idea what I'm talking about.'[10]

Denialism should not be countered using the methods of denialism. That means undercutting denialism's myth of the heroic Enlightenment truth-seeker. It also means acknowledging not just the ultimate values and moral positions underpinning one's arguments but also their limitations. As I've argued, part of what generates denialism is an unwillingness to face up to the consequences of one's desires. The global warming denialist's desire to maintain carbon-based capitalism refuses to acknowledge the suffering that this course of action would entail. As someone whose fervent desire is that we should transition as quickly as we can to a post-carbon economy, I have to acknowledge that there would be painful losses in this transition – I like plastic gadgets, long-haul holidays and fast cars as much as anyone. I just think those losses will be less painful than the alternative.

So yes, there are things that can be done to nurture trust in scholarship, to open up dialogue and wean

— *An Alternative* —

people off denialism. Yet denialism is still engrained in the modern world. Those denialisms that are supported and funded by states and corporations are certainly not going to go away soon. Even if they did, the Internet has endless dark corners where denialism can thrive. In any case, as we saw in the previous chapter, there are signs that, when denialism is being superseded, it is being superseded by something worse.

This possibility means that there is now no avoiding a reckoning with the discomfiting issues that those who fight denialism prefer to avoid: how do we respond to people who have radically different desires and morals to our own? How do we respond to people who delight in or are indifferent to genocide, to the suffering of millions, to venality and greed? We cannot assume that if people 'knew the truth' they would be like us. Denialism has hidden this moral diversity from us, but increasingly there is no hiding place.

Perhaps the default human attitude, to distant others at least, is one of apathy and selfishness. As Stanley Cohen suggests:

Instead of agonising about why denial occurs, we should take this state for granted. The theoretical problem is not 'why do we shut out?' but 'why do we ever not shut out?' The empirical problem is not to uncover yet more evidence of denial, but to discover the conditions under which information is acknowledged and acted upon. The political problem is how to create these conditions.[11]

— DENIAL —

Part of the problem is establishing what people really believe. Denialism, and the multitude of other ways that humans today bridge the gap, prevent a true accounting of moral diversity. It is hard to tell whether global warming denialists are secretly longing for the chaos and pain that global warming will bring, whether they are simply indifferent to it, or whether they would desperately like it not to be the case but are overwhelmed with desire to keep things as they are. It is hard to tell whether Holocaust deniers are preparing the ground for another genocide or whether they want to keep a pristine image of the goodness of the Nazis and the evil of the Jews. It is hard to tell whether an AIDS denialist who works to prevent Africans from having access to retrovirals is getting a kick out of their power over life and death or whether s/he is on a mission to save them from the evils of the West. In short, while denialism is an attempt to covertly legitimate an unspeakable desire, the nature of the denialist's understanding of the consequences of enacting that desire is usually unknowable.

Denialists are not alone in this. The assumption that humans possess coherent and static things called 'attitudes' or 'beliefs' has been undermined by research in psychology and sociology. Methodologies such as discourse analysis have demonstrated how attitudes only exist in the moment they are uttered.[12] The process of explaining and accounting for our attitudes is full of contradiction and improvisation. We are always

An Alternative

attempting to present our best side to the world. It is also true that when the limits of what is speakable are too narrow, language becomes so constrained that humans can lose any ability to give voice to their desires. The gap has meant that we have become slaves to language – and denialists are in the worst kind of bondage of all.

While we can assume that moral diversity does exist, we don't know its nature and extent. And what we cannot understand, we cannot fight. Should more and more former denialists take the denier's alternative, we will finally know where we stand. Instead of chasing shadows, we will be able to contemplate the stark moral choices we face.

This possibility opens up a new perspective on the vexed question of whether to publicly debate denialists. Denialists are constantly trying to position themselves as the 'other side' in a legitimate disagreement. Conceding this can be a very dangerous step. But we could rule out dialogue on 'the facts' and focus on deeper issues. Like Deborah Lipstadt, I would never publicly dialogue with David Irving on whether the gas chambers existed, but maybe a carefully moderated dialogue on more general questions, such as the ethics of violence and genocide, might be more productive. Perhaps offering to debate on such deeper questions might draw out denialists. Offering them a safe space in which to acknowledge their desires might allow them to emerge, blinking and stretching, into the light of moral acknowledgement.

Or, maybe, a safe space of this kind could pave the way for choosing a different moral path. Joshua Oppenheimer, in his 2012 documentary *The Act of Killing*, managed to create such a safe space for members of right-wing Indonesian death squads who committed multiple murders in the 1960s. While the film does allow them to express a lack of remorse and even pride in their killing, even getting them to act out their deeds, the same process eventually leads in some instances to disgust and self-loathing. The film shows that genuine repentance might be enabled not through forcing a particular morality on individuals, but through giving them the option to choose their own moral path.

Acknowledging who we are, what we want and what we have done is difficult. It also offers hope for a richer, more 'real' kind of empowerment than the ultimately illusory remaking of the world that denialists engage in. As Margaret Heffernan writes:

We make ourselves powerless when we choose not to know. But we give ourselves hope when we insist on looking. The very fact that wilful blindness is willed, that it is a product of a rich mix of experience, knowledge, thinking, neurons and neuroses, is what gives us the capacity to change it.[13]

Empowering and hopeful this prospect may be, but it is also horrifying. Can we really let genocide and

— *An Alternative* —

all sorts of other actions that have, for centuries, been ruled unspeakable, be opened up as speakable possibilities again? The problem is that just as the language of justification for such acts has been marginalised in modernity, so has the language of opposition. What would I say to David Irving other than 'genocide is wrong' or 'I'm a Jew, please don't kill me'? Theological, metaphysical and philosophical arguments against genocide might abound, but how effective are they when confronted by proud hatred?

Maybe we need a non-denier's alternative too. A non-denier's alternative would draw out denialists by engaging with their deeper desires and, simultaneously, would have traction with those who have taken the denier's alternative. Maybe such an alternative would be an appeal to self-interest. I'm not sure that I can convince someone who sees genocide as a legitimate act that such acts are always wrong. Perhaps I could at least get a hearing by pointing out the very real negative consequences of genocide for the genocidaire.

Here is what I could say to a Holocaust denier:

I understand that you believe that the Nazis were correct in attempting to wipe my people from the face of the earth. Maybe you also believe that there is a case for trying again. I know I can't convince you that, morally, the genocide of Jews or anyone else is an absolute wrong, in the past, in the present and in the future. Yet perhaps we can talk about the negative consequences of genocide for the perpetrators? And perhaps you might think about renouncing genocide in practice, even if you uphold it in theory? Genocide is not only hard work, it empowers some really distasteful people. The number of people who are capable of herding and killing large numbers of people is much smaller. As the Holocaust shows, previously decent genocidaires often suffer horribly and the indecent ones are empowered and cannot necessarily be controlled. In any case, might genocide not be a disappointment to you? Opposition to living, breathing Jews is at the centre of your very being. What would you do if we were not around? You need us more than we need you.

And here is what I could say to a global warming denialist:

I understand you want to keep our carbon-based capitalism alive as long as possible. But have you really thought through the consequences for you? You may think that you and the people you care about can be protected from the floods, the food shortages and the chaos, and maybe you can. Yet you are going to have to work hard to do this: you will have decades, or even centuries ahead of guarding borders against refugees, raising monumentally expensive dykes and ensuring food supplies against the starving billions. And in the end, your descendants (who will curse you) will still have to transition to a post-carbon economy once the oil runs out. You're probably too pessimistic about the possibilities of maintaining the scarcity and inequality on which capitalism is based in a post-carbon economy. Why not patent new energy technologies and charge crippling royalties to anyone who wants to use them? Why not find creative ways to make exploiting the sun and the wind as difficult and costly as exploiting oil and coal is now? Of course, I'll oppose you with every fibre of my being, but, frankly, I wouldn't bet against you winning. Let's have an open and fair fight!

Now these are arguments I haven't heard before! I don't know how or whether they would work. I do know that they do not rely on moral assumptions that may be untenable. The passive-aggressive tone is an honest tone in the way that post-denialism is honest. Perhaps it could shock and surprise denialists into a different, and more open, kind of dialogue?

I'm sure that many denialists would baulk at the prospect of trying to convince people of the rightness of genocide, environmental destruction and other such things. Denialism keeps a hidden coalition together – of those who long for the evils they deny and those who just don't want to face them – and who knows where the fainter hearts among them would jump if denialism disappeared? Those of us who are not denialists also have cause to worry. Are we confident that defenders of genocide wouldn't gain more adherents if they could openly advocate for their cause? Could an open and self-confident appeal that we should do

— DENIAL —

nothing about global warming regardless of the consequences for others actually increase the popularity of inaction as a strategy?

We don't know, we can't know until such ideas are tested in public.

All this raises issues of free speech and hate speech. How are Jews or other minorities supposed to tolerate open calls for them to be killed? Of course, we already face these issues now, albeit fogged by denialism. Liberating the desire of the denialist could mean eroding other freedoms – from persecution, from abuse. It is understandable that many want to deny a platform to those who espouse hate. I certainly have no wish to see celebrations of genocide and advocates of deliberate callousness to those at risk of environmental catastrophe, at universities, town halls and on street corners, let alone on Twitter. Yet we are no longer living in a world where 'no platforming' can ever be completely successful in a democracy: the online world is too anarchic and the boundaries between online and offline too porous. It is harder than ever to avoid encountering abhorrent arguments, and it is foolhardy not to prepare to counter them.

We also have to contend with the uncomfortable fact that restrictions on free speech can actually exacerbate denialism. The policing of racist language in recent decades has grown for very good and justifiable reasons: racist language intimidates, wounds and oppresses. At the same time, this policing has also

— *An Alternative* —

pushed those who might have otherwise used openly racist language to turn to more subterranean, allusive and insidious forms of racist expression.

One way of addressing these incredibly knotty dilemmas is to remember that denialism can never actually be 'free speech'. Denialists are not speaking freely: they are speaking under the weight of an unspeakable burden. Restricting denialism is therefore not restricting free speech. By enabling the truly free expression of desire while simultaneously restricting denialism we could make an offer to denialists: either say what you really want or forever be silent.

Maybe we as a species have been putting this test off for too long. Maybe it's time to find out what human beings are 'really' like. Maybe if we face up to who we are and what we desire we will surprise ourselves – in both good and bad ways. The short-term shock of witnessing the horrors of moral diversity could give way to a politics shorn of illusion and moral masquerade, where different visions of what it is to be human can openly contend. Might this not be a firmer base to rekindle a hope for human progress, based not on illusions of what we would like to be, but on an accounting for what we are?

– Notes –

Preface

1 Baigent, M., Lincoln, H., and Leigh, R., *The Holy Blood and the Holy Grail* (1982; London: Jonathan Cape).
2 Däniken, E. von, *Chariots of the Gods: Unsolved Mysteries of the Past* (1968; New York: Putnam).

1 The Failure

1 Sennett, R., *Together: The Rituals, Pleasures and Politics of Cooperation* (2012; London: Penguin), p.233.
2 Specter, M., *Denialism: How Irrational Thinking Hinders Scientific Progress, Harms the Planet, and Threatens Our Lives* (2010; Penguin: New York).
3 Chigwedere, P., Seage, G., Gruskin S., and Lee, T-H., 'Estimating the Lost Benefits of Antiretroviral Drug Use in South Africa', *Journal of Acquired Immune Deficiency Syndromes*, 49/4 (2008), pp.410–15.
4 Sun, L. H., 'Anti-Vaccine Activists Spark a State's Worst Measles Outbreak in Decades', *Washington Post*, 5 May 2017. https://www.washingtonpost.com/national/health-science/anti-vaccine-activists-spark-a-states-worst-measles-outbreak-in-decades/2017/05/04/a1fac952-2f39-11e7-9dec-764dc781686f_story.html.
5 Brannen, P., *The Ends of the World: Volcanic Apocalypses, Lethal Oceans, and Our Quest to Understand Earth's Past Mass Extinctions* (2017; London: HarperCollins); Mann, M. E., and Kump, L. R., *Dire Predictions: Understanding Climate Change* (2nd edn., 2015; London: Dorling Kindersley); Hansen, J., *Storms of My Grandchildren: The Truth about the Coming Climate*

Catastrophe and Our Last Chance to Save Humanity (2011; London: A&C Black).

6 Oreskes, N., and Conway, E. M., *Merchants of Doubt: How a Handful of Scientists Obscured the Truth on Issues from Tobacco Smoke to Global Warming* (2010; New York: Bloomsbury).

7 Storr, W., *The Heretics: Adventures with the Enemies of Science* (2013; London: Picador), p.10.

8 Evans, R. J., *Lying About Hitler: History, Holocaust and the David Irving Trial* (2001; New York: Basic Books).

9 Dawkins, R., *The God Delusion* (2007; London: Random House); Harris, S., *The End of Faith: Religion, Terror, and the Future of Reason* (2006; New York: Free Press); Hitchens, C., *God Is Not Great: How Religion Poisons Everything* (2007; New York: Warner Books).

10 Gray, J., *Black Mass: Apocalyptic Religion and the Death of Utopia* (2007; London: Penguin).

11 Gray, J., *Al Qaeda and What It Means to Be Modern* (2003; London: Faber and Faber).

12 Hind, D., *The Threat to Reason* (2007; London: Verso), p.4.

13 Jane, E. A., and Fleming, C., *Modern Conspiracy: The Importance of Being Paranoid* (2014; New York: Bloomsbury).

2 The Audacity of Denialism

1 Cohen, S., *States of Denial: Knowing About Atrocities and Suffering* (2001; Cambridge: Polity Press), p.24.

2 I am indebted to Stephen Frosh for his help in understanding psychoanalytic conceptions of denial.

3 Ronson, J., *The Psychopath Test* (2011; London: Pan Macmillan).

4 Sestero, G., and Bissell, T., *The Disaster Artist: My Life Inside The Room, the Greatest Bad Movie Ever Made* (2013; New York: Simon & Schuster).

5 Becker, E., *The Denial of Death* (1973; New York: Free Press).

6 Varki, A., and Brower, D., *Denial: Self-Deception, False Beliefs, and the Origins of the Human Mind* (2013; London: Hachette UK).

7 Frosh, S., 'The Re-Enactment of Denial', in Gulerce, A.

(ed.), *Re(con)figuring Psychoanalysis: Critical Juxtapositions of the Philosophical, the Sociohistorical and the Political* (2012; London: Palgrave), pp.60–75.

8 Zerubavel, E., *The Elephant in the Room: Silence and Denial in Everyday Life* (2006, Oxford: Oxford University Press), p.9.

9 Norgaard, K. M., *Living in Denial: Climate Change, Emotions, and Everyday Life* (2011; Cambridge MA: MIT Press) p.61.

10 Ibid., p.61.

11 See for example: Fourie, P., and Meyer, M., *The Politics of AIDS Denialism: South Africa's Failure to Respond* (2010; Farnham: Ashgate Publishing Ltd).

12 Specter, M., *Denialism: How Irrational Thinking Hinders Scientific Progress, Harms the Planet, and Threatens Our Lives* (2010; Penguin: New York), p.3.

13 Ibid., p.181.

14 Supran, G., and Oreskes, N., 'Assessing ExxonMobil's Climate Change Communications (1977–2014)', *Environmental Research Letters*, 12/8 (2017), 84019.

15 Stangneth, B., *Eichmann before Jerusalem: The Unexamined Life of a Mass Murderer* (2014; London: Bodley Head).

16 Ibid., p.298.

17 Ibid., p.309.

18 Oreskes, N., and Conway, E. M., *Merchants of Doubt: How a Handful of Scientists Obscured the Truth on Issues from Tobacco Smoke to Global Warming* (2010; New York: Bloomsbury).

19 Ibid.

20 Ibid., p.22.

21 'SMOKING AND HEALTH PROPOSAL' (1969; Brown & Williamson Records; Minnesota Documents). https://www.industrydocumentslibrary.ucsf.edu/tobacco/docs/psdw0147.

21 See, for example, 'Thomas Kuhn And The Catastrophic Climate Paradigm', *The Global Warming Policy Foundation: Opinions: Pros and Cons* (blog), 16 October 2010. https://www.thegwpf.com/thomas-kuhn-and-the-catastrophic-climate-paradigm/.

22 Faurisson, R., 'The adventure of revisionism', *The Journal of Historical Review*, 13/5 (1993), p.42. http://vho.org/GB/Journals/JHR/13/5/Faurisson42.html.

— Notes —

23 *The Mad Revisionist*, http://www.revisionism.nl/.
24 Phillips, M., *The World Turned Upside Down: The Global Battle over God, Truth, and Power* (2011; San Francisco and London: Encounter).
25 See, for example: Otto, S. L., *The War on Science: Who's Waging It, Why It Matters, What We Can Do About It* (2016; Minneapolis: Milkweed Editions) and Mooney, C., *The Republican War on Science* (new edn., 2006; New York: Basic Books).
26 See: https://junkscience.com/about/. Accessed 2 November 2017.
27 Op. cit., p.393.
28 For a flavour of the debate on whether denialism is postmodernism, see for example: Warner, J., 'Fact-Free Science', *New York Times*, 25 February 2011, https://www.nytimes.com/2011/02/27/magazine/27FOB-WWLN-t.html; Mooney, C., 'Once and For All: Climate Denial Is Not Postmodern', *DeSmogBlog*, 28 February 2011, https://www.desmogblog.com/once-and-all-climate-denial-not-postmodern.
29 Agin, D., *Junk Science: How Politicians, Corporations, and Other Hucksters Betray Us* (2006; New York: St Martin's Press).
30 Latour, B., *We Have Never Been Modern*, translated by Porter, C. (1993; Cambridge, MA: Harvard University Press).
31 Fuller, S., 'If There's a War, Please Direct Me to the Battlefield', in Mooney, C. (ed.), *Looking for a Fight: Is There a Republican War on Science?* (2006; West Lafayette: Parlor Press), p.58.
32 'About the IHR: Our Mission and Record', February 2017, accessed 2 November 2017, http://www.ihr.org/main/about.shtml.
33 Op. cit., p.185.
34 Op. cit., p.71.

3 Doing Denialism

1 Leuchter, F. A., *Auschwitz, the End of the Line: The Leuchter Report: The First Forensic Examination of Auschwitz* (1989; London: Focal Point Publications).

2 Ibid., p.29.
3 'The Leuchter Report: Gas Chambers Could Not Have Been Opened Safely in 20–30 Minutes?', n.d., The Nizkor Project, accessed 2 November 2017. http://www.nizkor.org/faqs/leuchter/leuchter-faq-06.html,
4 https://realitydrop.org/ Accessed 2 November 2017.
5 Sadly, it was never published.
6 See, for example: Diethelm, P., and McKee, M., 'Denialism: What Is It and How Should Scientists Respond?', *European Journal of Public Health* 19/1 (2009), pp.2–4; Hoofnagle, C. J., 'Denialists' Deck of Cards: An Illustrated Taxonomy of Rhetoric Used to Frustrate Consumer Protection Efforts', SSRN Scholarly Paper ID 962462 (2007; Rochester, NY: Social Science Research Network). https://papers.ssrn.com/abstract=962462.
7 Phillips, M., n.d. (first published 3 January 1996), 'How To Be A Revisionist Scholar', accessed 2 November 2017. https://www.jewishgen.org/ForgottenCamps/Exhib/HowtoEngl.html; 'Denier BS Bingo', The Skeptics Society Forum, 20 August 2016. http://www.skepticforum.com/viewtopic.php?f=39&t=27211; Terry, N., 'Denier Excuses For Their Epic Fail', *Holocaust Controversies* (blog), 5 August 2016. http://holocaustcontroversies.blogspot.com/2016/08/denier-excuses-for-their-epic-fail.html.
8 'The Ultimate Global Warming Challenge'; http://ultimateglobalwarmingchallenge.com/ Accessed 2 November 2017.
9 Summers, D., 'The evidence for vaccine safety is abundant. That will be $100,000, please', *Washington Post*, 7 February 2017; https://www.washingtonpost.com/news/to-your-health/wp/2017/02/17/the-evidence-for-vaccine-safety-is-abundant-that-will-be-100000-please/?utm_term=.aa34971db9f8.
10 'Orac', 'The Galileo Gambit', *Respectful Insolence* (blog), 21 February 2013. https://respectfulinsolence.com/2013/02/21/the-galileo-gambit/.
11 McKewon, E., 'Climate Deniers Intimidate Journal into Retracting Paper That Finds They Believe Conspiracy Theories', *Scientific American: The Conversation*, 3 April 2014. https://www.scientificamerican.com/article/climate-deniers-intimidate-

journal-into-retracting-paper-that-finds-they-believe-conspiracy-theories/.

12 'Beowulf and Grendel', n.d., *Creation Moments*; accessed 2 November 2017. http://www.creationmoments.com/content/beowulf-and-grendel.

13 One – highly educated – denialist made this argument to me. Really, I promise you, although I can barely believe it myself.

14 Shermer, M., and Grobman, A., *Denying History: Who Says The Holocaust Never Happened And Why Do They Say It?* (2000; Berkeley: University of California Press), pp.113–17.

15 One of the best collections of documents and analysis of the emails was produced by the *Guardian*: https://www.theguardian.com/environment/series/climate-wars-hacked-emails.

16 Boudry, M., and Braeckman, J., 'Immunizing Strategies and Epistemic Defense Mechanisms', *Philosophia* 39/1 (2011), pp.145–61. doi:10.1007/s11406-010-9254-9.

17 On the overwhelming nature of the consensus on anthropogenic climate change, see: Cook, J., et al., 'Consensus on Consensus: A Synthesis of Consensus Estimates on Human-Caused Global Warming', *Environmental Research Letters* 11/4 (2016), 48002. And on the small percentage are methodologically flawed: Benestad, R. E., et al., 'Learning from Mistakes in Climate Research', *Theoretical and Applied Climatology* 126/3–4 (2016), pp.699–703. doi:10.1007/s00704-015-1597-5.

18 'The Vaccine Package Insert Paradox', *The Logic of Science* (blog), 11 April 2017. https://thelogicofscience.com/2017/04/11/the-vaccine-package-insert-paradox/.

19 Bale, J. M., '"Conspiracy Theories" and Clandestine Politics', *Lobster*, June 1995. https://www.lobster-magazine.co.uk/articles/l29consp.htm.

20 Bale, J. M., 'Political Paranoia v. Political Realism: On Distinguishing between Bogus Conspiracy Theories and Genuine Conspiratorial Politics', *Patterns of Prejudice* 41/1 (2007), pp.45–60; Grimes, D. R., 'On the Viability of Conspiratorial Beliefs', *PLOS ONE* 11/1 (2016): e0147905.

21 For example: Ollier, C., n.d, 'Lysenko and Global Warming', The Lavoisier Group. Accessed 3 November 2017. http://

www.lavoisier.com.au/articles/greenhouse-science/method/ollier2008-28.php.

22 Mason, J., *Siege: The Collected Writings of James Mason*, edited by Jenkins, M. M. (2010; Bozeman, MT: Black Sun Publications), p.326.

23 Garland, B., 'Jews Pushing Hard for Mandatory "Holocaust Education" Laws – We Must Resist!', *Daily Stormer* (blog), 22 June 2016. https://www.dailystormer.com/jews-pushing-hard-for-mandatory-holocaust-education-laws-we-must-resist/.

24 Charny, I. W., 'The Psychology of Denial of Known Genocides', in *Genocide: A Critical Bibliographic Review*, volume 2, edited by. Charny, I. W. (1991; London: Mansell Publishing) pp.3–37.

25 Quoted in Levi, P., *The Drowned and the Saved* (1988; New York: Simon & Schuster), pp.11-12.

4 The Gap

1 Translation adapted from *The JPS Hebrew–English Tanakh* (2000; Philadelphia: Jewish Publication Society).

2 A full transcript of the stele can be found here: http://www.ancientegyptonline.co.uk/sisrael.html.

3 Julius Caesar, *The Gallic Wars*, translated by McDevitte, W. A., and Bohn, W. S. (1869), ch. 24.

4 Kiernan, B., *Blood and Soil: A World History of Genocide and Extermination from Sparta to Darfur* (2007; New Haven: Yale University Press); Day, D., *Conquest: How Societies Overwhelm Others* (2008; Oxford: Oxford University Press).

5 For a discussion of the source and veracity of this famous quote, see: 'What Was the Context of This Famous Genghis Khan Quote?', History Stack Exchange, 14 August 2015. https://history.stackexchange.com/questions/23975/what-was-the-context-of-this-famous-genghis-khan-quote.

6 Quoted in Boobbyer, P., *The Stalin Era* (2000; London: Routledge) p.102.

7 Pinker, S., *The Better Angels of Our Nature: The Decline of Violence in History and Its Causes* (2011; London: Penguin); Pinker, S., *Enlightenment Now: The Case for Reason, Science,*

— *Notes* —

Humanism and Progress (2018; London: Penguin)

8 Diamond, J., *Collapse: How Societies Choose to Fail or Survive* (2005; London: Allen Lane), p.114.

9 As this book was close to completion, I was made aware that some scholars have contested the story of the Easter Island collapse, arguing that the real collapse occurred following 'discovery' by the West. However, the contrast between the broad awareness of the consequences of our actions in modernity, and the more limited awareness in the pre-modern era remains valid. See Middleton, G. D., 'What the Idea of Civilisational "Collapse" Says about History', Aeon, 16 November 2017. https://aeon.co/essays/what-the-idea-of-civilisational-collapse-says-about-history.

10 Fukuyama, F., *The End of History and the Last Man* (1992; New York: Free Press).

11 Runciman, D., *Political Hypocrisy: The Mask of Power, from Hobbes to Orwell and Beyond* (2009; Princeton: Princeton University Press).

12 Seu, I. B., *Passivity Generation: Human Rights and Everyday Morality* (2013; Basingstoke: Palgrave Macmillan).

13 Ibid., p.199.

14 Foucault, M., *Discipline and Punish: The Birth of the Prison*, translated by Sheridan, A. (1977; London: Penguin).

15 Choi-Fitzpatrick, A., *What Slaveholders Think: How Contemporary Perpetrators Rationalize What They Do* (2017; New York: Columbia University Press).

16 Frank, T., *What's the Matter with Kansas?: How Conservatives Won the Heart of America* (2005; New York: Henry Holt).

17 Latour, B., *We Have Never Been Modern*, translated by Porter, C. (1993; Cambridge, MA: Harvard University Press).

18 Moore, J., *Capitalism in the Web of Life: Ecology and the Accumulation of Capital* (2015; London: Verso).

19 Lewandowsky, S., Oberauer, K., and Gignac, E. G., 'NASA Faked the Moon Landing – Therefore, (Climate) Science Is a Hoax: An Anatomy of the Motivated Rejection of Science', *Psychological Science* 24/5 (2013), pp.622–33. doi:10.1177/0956797612457686.

20 Kahan, D. M., Braman, D., Gastil, J., Slovic, P., and Mertz, C.

K., 'Culture and Identity-Protective Cognition: Explaining the White Male Effect in Risk Perception', SSRN Scholarly Paper ID 995634 (2007; Rochester, NY: Social Science Research Network). https://papers.ssrn.com/abstract=995634; McCright, A. M., and Dunlap, R. E., 'Cool Dudes: The Denial of Climate Change among Conservative White Males in the United States', *Global Environmental Change* 21/4 (2011), pp.1163–72.

21 Rubin, E. L., 'Rejecting Climate Change: Not Science Denial, but Regulation Phobia', SSRN Scholarly Paper ID 2900352 (2017; Rochester, NY: Social Science Research Network). https://papers.ssrn.com/abstract=2900352.

22 Davidson, H., 'Oil Company Santos Admits Business Plan Is Based on 4C Temperature Rise', *Guardian*, 5 May 2017. http://www.theguardian.com/environment/2017/may/05/santos-admits-business-plan-based-4c-global-temperature-rise; Supran, G., and Oreskes, N., 'Assessing ExxonMobil's Climate Change Communications (1977–2014)', *Environmental Research Letters* 12/8 (2017): 84019. doi:10.1088/1748-9326/aa815f.

23 Papsco, N., 'North Carolina Denies and Defies Science in House Bill 819', *Columbia Undergraduate Law Review* (blog), 21 March 2016. http://blogs.cuit.columbia.edu/culr/2016/03/21/north-carolina-denies-and-defies-science-in-house-bill-819/.

24 Mooney, C., 'The Strange Relationship between Global Warming Denial and ... Speaking English', *Mother Jones*, 22 July 2014. http://www.motherjones.com/environment/2014/07/climate-denial-us-uk-australia-canada-english/.

25 Schlögel, K., *Moscow, 1937*, translated by Livingstone, R. (2012; Cambridge: Polity Press)

26 Lim, L., *The People's Republic of Amnesia: Tiananmen Revisited* (2014; Oxford: Oxford University Press).

27 I didn't buy it, something I regret for no other reason than that I cannot find the details of this book online.

28 Martin, A., 'The Prosecution's Case Against DNA', *New York Times*, 25 November 2011. https://www.nytimes.com/2011/11/27/magazine/dna-evidence-lake-county.html.

29 Goldberg, D. T., *Are We All Postracial Yet?* (2015; Cambridge: Polity Press), pp.74–5.

30 Dijk, T. A. van, 'Discourse and the Denial of Racism', *Discourse & Society* 3/1 (1992), p.116.
31 Rich, D., *The Left's Jewish Problem: Jeremy Corbyn, Israel and Anti-Semitism* (2016; London: Biteback Publishing).

5 Predicament and Pathos

1 Fourie, P., and Meyer, M., *The Politics of AIDS Denialism: South Africa's Failure to Respond* (2010; Farnham: Ashgate Publishing Ltd), p.126.
2 For the case that atrocities in Bosnia constituted genocide, see for example: Cigar, N., *Genocide in Bosnia: The Policy of 'Ethnic Cleansing'* (1995; College Station: Texas A&M University Press).
3 Monbiot, G., 'How did genocide denial become a doctrine of the internationalist left?', *Guardian*, 22 May 2012.
4 Johnson, C., 'Pamela Geller, Genocide Denier', *Little Green Footballs* (blog), 6 April 2011. http://littlegreenfootballs.com/article/38672_Pamela_Geller_Genocide_Denier.
5 Cahalan, P., 'David Bellamy: "I Was Shunned. They Didn't Want to Hear."' *Independent*, 13 January 2013. http://www.independent.co.uk/news/people/profiles/david-bellamy-i-was-shunned-they-didnt-want-to-hear-8449307.html.
6 Park, R., *Voodoo Science: The Road from Foolishness to Fraud* (2000; Oxford: Oxford University Press), p.10.
7 For an accessible summary of some recent research in this area, see: Kolbert, E., 'Why Facts Don't Change Our Minds', *New Yorker*, 20 February 2017. https://www.newyorker.com/magazine/2017/02/27/why-facts-dont-change-our-minds.
8 Haidt, J., *The Righteous Mind: Why Good People Are Divided by Politics and Religion* (2012; New York: Pantheon Books), p.21.
9 Gorman, S. E., and Gorman, J. M., *Denying to the Grave: Why We Ignore the Facts That Will Save Us* (2016; Oxford, New York: Oxford University Press), p.13.
10 Festinger, L., Riecken, H. W., and Schachter, S., *When Prophecy Fails* (2008; London: Pinter & Martin).
11 Nyhan, B., and Reifler, J., 'When Corrections Fail: The Persistence of Political Misperceptions', *Political Behavior* 32/2

(2010), pp.303–30.

12 Shermer, M., 'Confessions of a Former Environmental Skeptic', *Michael Shermer* (blog), 15 April 2008. https://michaelshermer.com/2008/04/confessions-of-a-former-environmental-skeptic/.

13 Muller, R. A., 'The Conversion of a Climate-Change Skeptic', *New York Times*, 28 July 2012. https://www.nytimes.com/2012/07/30/opinion/the-conversion-of-a-climate-change-skeptic.html.

14 Limbaugh, R., 'God and Climate Change', *The Rush Limbaugh Show*, 3 November 2015. https://www.rushlimbaugh.com/daily/2015/11/03/god_and_climate_change/.

15 See for example: Hoffman, D. L., and Simmons, A., *The Resilient Earth: Science, Global Warming and the Future of Humanity* (2008; Charleston: BookSurge Publishing).

16 Moore, S., 'America's Infinite Resource: Oil', *Christian Broadcast News* (blog), 28 August 2015. http://www1.cbn.com/cbnnews/finance/2015/August/Americas-Infinite-Resource-Oil.

17 Brogan, K., 'Homebirth: The Opportunity of a Lifetime', 25 April 2017. http://kellybroganmd.com/homebirth-the-opportunity-of-a-lifetime/.

18 Sereny, G., *Into That Darkness: From Mercy Killing to Mass Murder* (1974; London: André Deutsch).

19 'Sobibor Survivor Thomas Tovi Blatt Confronts Death Camp Commandant Karl Frenzel (Forced Labour Section) in 1983', n.d., Holocaust Education and Archive Research Team. Accessed 3 November 2017. http://www.holocaustresearchproject.org/survivor/blattfrenzel.html.

20 'Himmler's 10/04/43 Posen Speech', n.d., The Nizkor Project. Accessed 3 November 2017. http://www.nizkor.org/hweb/people/h/himmler-heinrich/posen/oct-04-43/.

21 Mandel, K., 'How Do You Spot a Climate Science Denial Blog? Check the Polar Bears', *DeSmog UK* (blog), 1 December 2017. https://www.desmog.uk/2017/12/01/how-do-you-spot-climate-science-denial-blog-check-polar-bears.

22 Leuchter, F. A., *Auschwitz, the End of the Line: The Leuchter Report: The First Forensic Examination of Auschwitz* (1989; London: Focal Point Publications).

— *Notes* —

23 Gardell, M., *Gods of the Blood: The Pagan Revival and White Separatism* (2003; Durham: Duke University Press), p.180.

6 The Denier's Alternative

1 Beisner, E. C., 'The Biblical Perspective of Environmental Stewardship: Subduing and Ruling the Earth to the Glory of God and the Benefit of Our Neighbors', Cornwall Alliance, 2013. http://cornwallalliance.org/landmark-documents/the-biblical-perspective-of-environmental-stewardship-subduing-and-ruling-the-earth-to-the-glory-of-god-and-the-benefit-of-our-neighbors/.

2 Coulter, A., 'Oil Good; Democrats Bad', *Townhall*, 12 October 2000. https://townhall.com/columnists/anncoulter/2000/10/12/oil-good;-democrats-bad-n850347.

3 Zycher, B., 'Springtime for the Rockefellers', American Enterprise Institute, 30 March 2016. https://www.aei.org/publication/springtime-for-the-rockefellers/.

4 Epstein, A., *The Moral Case for Fossil Fuels* (2014; London: Penguin), p.13.

5 Rand, A., 'Environmentalism: The Anti-Industrial Revolution' (originally published 1970). Downloaded 2 November 2017 from: https://assets.documentcloud.org/documents/1630044/societyforo00014.pdf: p.10.

6 Ben-Ami, D., 'Beware Greens in Progressive Clothing', Spiked, 22 April 2016. http://www.spiked-online.com/newsite/article/beware-greens-in-progressive-clothing/18044.

7 Williams, C., 'Rothbard Explains the Proper Response to Climate Change', Text. Mises Institute, 9 March 2017. https://mises.org/blog/rothbard-explains-proper-response-climate-change.

8 Capella, F., 'The Ethics of Freedom and Climate Change', Mises Institute, 30 October 2009. https://mises.org/library/ethics-freedom-and-climate-change.

9 Milloy, S., 'I Fought ExxonMobil Management on Climate – and I Won', *JunkScience.com* (blog), 13 March 2017. https://junkscience.com/2017/03/i-fought-exxonmobil-management-on-climate-and-i-won/.

10 Carlin, A., 'How Your Tax Dollars May Save Energy but End Up

Penalizing Homeowners', Heartland Institute, 7 August 2017. https://www.heartland.org/news-opinion/news/how-your-tax-dollars-may-save-energy-but-end-up-penalizing-homeowners.

11 Goklany, I. M., 'The Pontifical Academies' Broken Moral Compass', GWPF Briefing 19 (2015; London: Global Warming Policy Foundation), p.18.

12 Lawson, N., 'The Trouble with Climate Change', GWPF Essay 1 (2014; London: Global Warming Policy Foundation), p.11.

13 Mills, D., '"The Maldives Might Disappear but We Shouldn't Be Building Windmills and All That Rubbish": Rupert Murdoch Shares His Views on Climate Change', *Daily Mail*, 14 July 2014. http://www.dailymail.co.uk/news/article-2690828/The-Maldives-disappear-News-Corporation-boss-Rupert-Murdoch-says-climate-change-real-cares-sea-level-rises-wipe-Maldives.html.

14 Beisner, 'The Biblical Perspective'.

15 Seo, S. N., 'Helping Low-Latitude, Poor Countries with Climate Change', *Regulation*, Winter 2015: 6.

16 Harsanyi, D., 'Great News! Americans Don't Really Care About Climate Change', *The Federalist*, 20 November 2015. http://thefederalist.com/2015/11/20/great-news-americans-dont-really-care-about-climate-change/.

17 O'Neil, B., 'Public Apathy on Climate Change Is a Cause for Celebration, Not Concern', *SPPI Blog* (blog), 17 March 2015. http://sppiblog.org/news/public-apathy-on-climate-change-is-a-cause-for-celebration-not-concern.

18 O'Neill, B., 'Greens Are the Enemies of Liberty', *Guardian*, 15 July 2008. http://www.theguardian.com/commentisfree/2008/jul/15/climatechange.

19 Delingpole, J., 'Climate Change: The Greatest-Ever Conspiracy Against The Taxpayer', *Breitbart* (blog), 28 March 2016. http://www.breitbart.com/london/2016/03/28/climate-change-the-biggest-conspiracy-against-the-taxpayer-in-history/.

20 Erickson, E., 'I Simply Do Not Care About Global Warming', *Red State*, 27 August 2014. https://www.redstate.com/erick/2014/08/27/i-simply-do-not-care-about-global-warming/.

21 Carrington, A., n.d. 'The Solution to the Synagogue of Satan', The Official Website Of Andrew Carrington Hitchcock.

Accessed 6 November 2017. http://andrewcarringtonhitchcock.com/the-solution-to-the-synagogue-of-satan/.

22 Carrington, A., 'From Genesis to Genocide – Destiny of the Jews', The Official Website Of Andrew Carrington Hitchcock, 9 February 2015. http://andrewcarringtonhitchcock.com/blog/from-genesis-to-genocide-destiny-of-the-jews.

23 'A Century of Deceit: Iraq, the World Wars, Holocaust Mythology and Zionist Militarism', Non-Aligned Media, 10 April 2015. http://nonalignedmedia.com/2015/04/a-century-of-deceit-iraq-the-world-wars-holocaust-mythology-and-zionist-militarism/.

24 'Irving v. Lipstadt Judgment – Part IX', n.d., Nizkor Project. Accessed 6 November 2017. http://www.nizkor.org/hweb/people/i/irving-david/judgment-09-01.html.

25 Braun, F., 'Why are Jews Persecuted?', post on CODOH (Committee for Open Debate on the Holocaust) Forum, 15 January 2009. Quoted in: Romanov, S., 'What the CODOHites Are Saying When They Think Nobody Is Watching', *Holocaust Controversies*, 1 May 2017. http://holocaustcontroversies.blogspot.com/2017/05/what-codohites-are-saying-when-they.html.

26 Post by 'littlefieldJohn' on VNN Forum 1 July 2015 https://vnnforum.com/showthread.php?t=278553

27 Truthwillout, '10 Reasons Why Hitler Was One of the Good Guys: The Greatest Story Never Told', 4 May 2014. https://thegreateststorynevertold.tv/10-reasons-why-hitler-was-one-of-the-good-guys/.

28 Quoted in: Romanov, S., 'Another "somewhat honest" denier', 25 November 2006. http://holocaustcontroversies.blogspot.com/2006/11/another-somewhat-honest-denier.html.

29 Garland, B., 'The Hitler Question', *Daily Stormer*, 20 April 2017. https://www.dailystormer.com/the-hitler-question/.

30 'Good Jews, Bad Jews and Zionism', White Aryan Resistance, 24 February 2015. http://www.resistance88.com/topics/demographics/problem/goodbad1.htm#.WgCG1BN-rxl.

31 Faurisson, R., 'The Victories of Revisionism', *Robert Faurisson Unofficial Blog*, 11 December 2006. http://robertfaurisson.

blogspot.com/2006/12/victories-of-revisionism.html.
32 MacDonald, A., *The Turner Diaries* (1978; National Vanguard Books), p.72.

7 The Post-Denialist Age

1 For a thorough explanation and debunking of intelligent design, see: Shermer, M., *Why Darwin Matters: The Case Against Intelligent Design* (2006; New York: Times Books).
2 See the following website which exposes and challenges this soft denialism: http://defendinghistory.com/.
3 Lomborg, B., *The Skeptical Environmentalist: Measuring the Real State of the World* (2001; Cambridge: Cambridge University Press).
4 Friel, H., *The Lomborg Deception: Setting the Record Straight About Global Warming* (2010; New Haven: Yale University Press).
5 Ridley, M., *The Rational Optimist: How Prosperity Evolves* (2010; London: HarperCollins UK).
6 Epstein, A., *The Moral Case for Fossil Fuels* (2014; London: Penguin).
7 Banerjee, N., 'How Big Oil Lost Control of Its Climate Misinformation Machine', InsideClimate News, 22 December 2017. https://insideclimatenews.org/news/22122017/big-oil-heartland-climate-science-misinformation-campaign-koch-api-trump-infographic.
8 Delingpole, J., 'Why I Totally Hate Big Oil – And Why You Should Too…', *Breitbart*, 14 March 2017. http://www.breitbart.com/big-government/2017/03/14/delingpole-why-i-totally-hate-big-oil-and-why-you-should-too/.
9 D'Ancona, M., *Post-Truth: The New War on Truth and How to Fight Back* (2017; Ebury Digital); Ball, J., *Post-Truth: How Bullshit Conquered the World* (2017; London: Biteback Publishing); Davis, E., *Post-Truth: Why We Have Reached Peak Bullshit and What We Can Do About It* (2017; London: Little, Brown Book Group).
10 For a voluminous debunking of the 9/11 truth movement, see:

Dunbar, D., and Brad Reagan, B.,. 2011. *Debunking 9/11 Myths: Why Conspiracy Theories Can't Stand Up to the Facts* (2006; New York: Hearst Books).

11 Garwood, C., *Flat Earth: The History of an Infamous Idea* (2008; London: Pan Macmillan).

12 Kriss, S., 'My Journey to the Centre of the Flat Earth Conspiracy', *Vice*, 15 February 2016. https://www.vice.com/en_uk/article/zngdg3/the-earth-is-flat-sam-kriss?utm_campaign=global&utm_medium=ctabutton&utm_source=vicefbuk.

13 Garland, D., 'Death, Denial, Discourse: On the Forms and Functions of American Capital Punishment', in *Crime, Social Control and Human Rights: From Moral Panics to States of Denial, Essays in Honour of Stanley Cohen*, edited by Downes, D., Rock, P., Chinkin, C., and Gearty, C., pp.136–56 (2013; Portland, OR: Willan Publishing), p.148.

14 Norton, B., 'Libertarian superstar Ayn Rand defended Native American genocide: "Racism didn't exist in this country until the liberals brought it up"', *Salon*, 14 October 2015. http://www.salon.com/2015/10/14/libertarian_superstar_ayn_rand_defended_genocide_of_savage_native_americans/; Rand, A., 'Environmentalism: The Anti-Industrial Revolution' (originally published 1970), Downloaded 2 November 2017 from https://assets.documentcloud.org/documents/1630044/societyforo00014.pdf.

15 Burns, J., *Goddess of the Market: Ayn Rand and the American Right* (2009; New York: Oxford University Press).

16 Hughes, B., 'Dick Cheney Says U.S. Did Not Torture Terror Suspects', 14 December 2014. *Washington Examiner*. http://www.washingtonexaminer.com/dick-cheney-says-us-did-not-torture-terror-suspects/article/2557376.

17 Mitchell, J. E., and Harlow, B., *Enhanced Interrogation: Inside the Minds and Motives of the Islamic Terrorists Trying To Destroy America* (2016; New York: Crown Publishing Group).

18 Jacobs, B., 'Donald Trump on Waterboarding: "Even If It Doesn't Work They Deserve It"', *The Guardian*, 24 November 2015. http://www.theguardian.com/us-news/2015/nov/24/

donald-trump-on-waterboarding-even-if-it-doesnt-work-they-deserve-it.

19 Suskind, R., 'Faith, Certainty and the Presidency of George W. Bush', *New York Times*, 17 October 2004. https://www.nytimes.com/2004/10/17/magazine/faith-certainty-and-the-presidency-of-george-w-bush.html.

20 Milman, O., and Morris, S., 'Trump Is Deleting Climate Change, One Site at a Time', *Guardian*, 14 May 2017. http://www.theguardian.com/us-news/2017/may/14/donald-trump-climate-change-mentions-government-websites; Zhang, S., 'Looking Back at Canada's Political Fight Over Science', *The Atlantic*, 26 January 2017. https://www.theatlantic.com/science/archive/2017/01/canada-war-on-science/514322/.

21 Mooney, C., *The Republican War on Science* (new edn. 2006; New York: Basic Books).

22 Phillips, M., *The World Turned Upside Down: The Global Battle over God, Truth, and Power* (2011; San Francisco and London: Encounter) p. xvi.

23 Devji, F., n.d., 'Beyond Right or Wrong, beyond Fact or Fake, Lies Sincerity', Aeon. Accessed 3 November 2017. https://aeon.co/essays/beyond-right-or-wrong-beyond-fact-or-fake-lies-sincerity.

24 I am grateful to Rio Goldhammer for introducing me to the concept of kayfabe. See also: Rogers, N., 'How Wrestling Explains Alex Jones and Donald Trump.' *New York Times*, 25 April 2017. https://www.nytimes.com/2017/04/25/opinion/wrestling-explains-alex-jones-and-donald-trump.html?nytmobile=0.

25 See, for example: Fluss, H., and Frim, L., 'Aliens, Antisemitism, and Academia', Jacobin, 11 March 2017. http://jacobinmag.com/2017/03/jason-reza-jorjani-stony-brook-alt-right-arktos-continental-philosophy-modernity-enlightenment/.

26 Jane, E. A., and Fleming, C., *Modern Conspiracy: The Importance of Being Paranoid* (2014; New York: Bloomsbury Publishing) pp.53–4.

27 Terry, N., 2017. 'Holocaust Denial in the Age of Web 2.0 Negationist Discourse since the Irving-Lipstadt Trial', in Behrens,

P., Jensen, O., and Terry, N., eds., *Holocaust and Genocide Denial: A Contextual Perspective*, pp.34–54 (2017; Abingdon: Routledge) p.53.

28 Weber, M., 'How Relevant Is Holocaust Revisionism?', Institute for Historical Review, 7 January 2009. http://www.ihr.org/weber_revisionism_jan09.html.

29 Terry, N., 'Eric Hunt Is No Longer a Holocaust Denier', *Holocaust Controversies* (blog), 14 February 2017. http://holocaustcontroversies.blogspot.com/2017/02/eric-hunt-is-no-longer-holocaust-denier.html.

30 Weber, 'How Relevant Is Holocaust Revisionism?'.

31 Quoted in Terry, *Holocaust and Genocide Denial*.

32 For a good summary of the controversy, see: Nelson, L., 'The Controversy over the White House Holocaust Statement, Explained', *Vox*, 30 January 2017. https://www.vox.com/2017/1/30/14431216/trump-holocaust-statement-6-million-jews.

33 Novick, P., *The Holocaust and Collective Memory* (1999; London: Bloomsbury Publishing).

34 Goldberg, J., 'A Brief Introduction to Pro-Holocaust Twitter', *The Atlantic*, 8 June 2016. https://www.theatlantic.com/politics/archive/2016/06/welcome-to-nazi-twitter-ill-be-your-guide/486233/.

35 Atzmon, G., 'Truth, History and Integrity by Gilad Atzmon', *Gilad Atzmon: Thoughts* (blog), 13 March 2010. http://www.gilad.co.uk/writings/truth-history-and-integrity-by-gilad-atzmon.html.

36 Yakowicz, W., 'His Jewish Problem', *Tablet Magazine*, 16 March 2011. http://www.tabletmag.com/jewish-news-and-politics/67305/his-jewish-problem.

37 Pomerantsev, P., *Nothing Is True and Everything Is Possible: Adventures in Modern Russia* (2015; London: Faber & Faber).

38 Nagle, A., *Kill All Normies: Online Culture Wars From 4Chan And Tumblr To Trump And The Alt-Right* (2017; Alresford: John Hunt Publishing), pp.31–2.

39 Pomerantsev, P., 'Why We're Post-Fact', *Granta Magazine*, 20 July 2016. https://granta.com/why-were-post-fact/.

40 Nagle, A., 'Goodbye, Pepe', *The Baffler*, 15 August 2017. https://thebaffler.com/latest/goodbye-pepe.
41 Penny, L., 'On the Milo Bus With the Lost Boys of America's New Right', *Pacific Standard*, 22 February 2017. https://psmag.com/news/on-the-milo-bus-with-the-lost-boys-of-americas-new-right.
42 Quoted in: Fenton, J., 'Duterte's Last Hurrah: On the Road to Martial Law', *New York Review of Books*, 23 February 2017. http://www.nybooks.com/articles/2017/02/23/duterte-philippines-road-to-martial-law/.
43 Ibid.
44 Reuters, 'Donald Trump Tells Duterte: "You're Doing a Great Job", Philippines Claims', *Guardian*, 3 May 2017. http://www.theguardian.com/world/2017/may/03/trump-tells-duterte-youre-doing-a-great-job-philippines-claims.
45 Kahn-Harris, K., *Extreme Metal: Music and Culture on the Edge* (2006; Oxford: Berg).
46 See, for example, underground musician and writer Boyd Rice's paean to rape: Rice, B., 'Revolt Against Penis Envy', *GIVE ME FIVE BEES FOR A QUARTER* (blog), 19 February 2009. https://idabby.wordpress.com/2009/02/19/43/.
47 Gray, R., 'Behind the Internet's Anti-Democracy Movement', *The Atlantic*, 10 February 2017. https://www.theatlantic.com/politics/archive/2017/02/behind-the-internets-dark-anti-democracy-movement/516243/.
48 Schmidt, S., 'KKK Leader Threatens to "burn" Latina Journalist, the First Black Person on His Property', *Washington Post*, 21 August 2017. https://www.washingtonpost.com/news/morning-mix/wp/2017/08/21/kkk-leader-threatens-to-burn-latina-journalist-the-first-black-person-on-his-property/?utm_term=.92ef2c911be1.
49 'Charlottesville 2.0: Be There or Be Square', *Daily Stormer*. 5 August 2017. https://www.dailystormer.com/charlottesville-2-0-be-there-or-be-square/.
50 Feinberg, A., 'This Is The Daily Stormer's Playbook', HuffPost UK, 13 December 2017. http://www.huffingtonpost.com/entry/daily-stormer-nazi-style-guide_us_5a2ece19e4b0ce3b344492f2.

8 An Alternative

1. Monbiot, G., 'The Trouble with Trusting Complex Science', *Guardian*, 8 March 2010. http://www.theguardian.com/commentisfree/cif-green/2010/mar/08/belief-in-climate-change-science.
2. Rensin, E., 'The Blathering Superego at the End of History', *Los Angeles Review of Books*, 18 June 2017. https://lareviewofbooks.org/article/the-blathering-superego-at-the-end-of-history/.
3. Scranton, R., *Learning to Die in the Anthropocene: Reflections on the End of a Civilization* (2015; San Francisco: City Lights Publishers) p.16.
4. Kingsnorth, P., 'The Quants and the Poets', 21 April 2011. http://paulkingsnorth.net/2011/04/21/the-quants-and-the-poets/.
5. Westen, D., *The Political Brain: The Role of Emotion in Deciding the Fate of the Nation* (2008; London: Hachette UK).
6. Wood, T., and Porter, E., 'The Elusive Backfire Effect: Mass Attitudes' Steadfast Factual Adherence', SSRN Scholarly Paper ID 2819073 (2017; Rochester, NY: Social Science Research Network). https://papers.ssrn.com/abstract=2819073.
7. Cook, J., Lewandowsky, S., and Ecker, U. K. H., 'Neutralizing Misinformation through Inoculation: Exposing Misleading Argumentation Techniques Reduces Their Influence', *PLOS ONE* 12/5 (2017): e0175799.
8. Gorman, S. E., and Gorman, J. M., *Denying to the Grave: Why We Ignore the Facts That Will Save Us* (2016; New York: Oxford University Press), pp.243–66.
9. Siegel, E., '22 Messages of Hope (and Science) for Creationists', *Starts With A Bang!* (blog), 6 February 2014. https://medium.com/starts-with-a-bang/22-messages-of-hope-and-science-for-creationists-8712e42fbb0d.
10. Jane, E. A., and Fleming, C., *Modern Conspiracy: The Importance of Being Paranoid* (2014; Bloomsbury Publishing), p.138.
11. Cohen, S., *States of Denial: Knowing About Atrocities and Suffering* (2001; Cambridge: Polity Press), p.249.

12 Potter, J., and Wetherell, M., *Discourse and Social Psychology: Beyond Attitudes and Behaviour* (1987; London: Sage Publications).
13 Heffernan, M., *Wilful Blindness: Why We Ignore the Obvious at Our Peril* (2007; London: Simon and Schuster), p.331.

Other titles from Notting Hill Editions*

A Short History of Power
by Simon Heffer

Taking a panoramic view from the days of Thucydides to the present, Heffer analyses the motive forces behind the pursuit of power, and explains in a beautiful argument why history is destined to repeat itself.

'Heffer's admirably steely tract combines a well-informed historical intelligence with a subtle account of 2,500 years of Western history.' – *Times Literary Supplement*

The Mystery of Being Human: God, Freedom and the NHS
by Raymond Tallis

In his latest collection of essays, author, physician and humanist philosopher Raymond Tallis meditates on the complexity of human consciousness, free will, mathematics, God and eternity. The philosophical reflections are interrupted by a fierce polemic 'Lord Howe's Wicked Dream', in which Tallis exposes the 'institutionally corrupt' deception intended to destroy the NHS.

Pilgrims of the Air: The Passing of the Passenger Pigeons
by John Wilson Foster

This is the story of the rapid and brutal extinction of the Passenger Pigeon, once so abundant that they 'blotted out the sky', until the last bird died on 1st September, 1914. It is also an evocative story of wild America – the astonishment that accompanied its discovery, the allure of its natural 'productions', its ruthless exploitation, and a morality tale for our times.

CLASSIC COLLECTION

The Classic Collection brings together the finest essayists of the past, introduced by contemporary writers.

A Roundabout Manner – Sketches of Life by W.M. Thackeray
Introduced by John Sutherland

The Russian Soul – Selections from a Writer's Diary by Fyodor Dostoevsky
Introduced by Rosamund Bartlett

Drawn from Life – Selected Essays of Michel de Montaigne
Introduced by Tim Parks

Grumbling at Large – Selected Essays of J. B. Priestley
Introduced by Valerie Grove

Beautiful and Impossible Things – Selected Essays of Oscar Wilde
Introduced by Gyles Brandreth

Words of Fire – Selected Essays of Ahad Ha'am
Introduced by Brian Klug

Essays on the Self – Selected Essays of Virginia Woolf
Introduced by Joanna Kavenna

All That is Worth Remembering – Selected Essays of William Hazlitt
Introduced by Duncan Wu

*All NHE titles are available in the UK, and some titles are available in the rest of the world. For more information, please visit www.nottinghilleditions.com.

A selection of our titles is distributed in the US and Canada by New York Review Books. For more information on available titles, please visit www.nyrb.com.